MW00413417

SMALL BUSINESS TAX DEDUCTIONS REVEALED

29 TAX-SAVING TIPS YOU WISH YOU KNEW (FOR SELF-EMPLOYED PEOPLE ONLY)

SMALL BUSINESS TAX TIPS, VOLUME 1

WAYNE DAVIES, EA

Get 3 Free Tax-Saving Gifts at
SelfEmployedTaxDeductionsToday.com

#1: Tax-Saving Guide for Small Businesses
#2: Small Business Tax Tips Newsletter
#3: $150 Worth of Tax Coupons

TABLE OF CONTENTS

FREE GIFTS

I've included these special bonuses for you.

Free Newsletter
Visit www.SelfEmployedTaxDeductionsToday.com to subscribe. You'll receive easy-to-understand tax tips delivered to your inbox every week.

Free Report
When you subscribe to my newsletter, you'll also get Free Instant Access to my Tax-Saving Guide, "Top 10 Tax Deductions for Small Business Owners & Self-Employed People".

Free Tax Coupons Worth $150
These coupons include a 30-minute phone consultation with me and a confidential review of your most recently filed income returns (business and personal), at no charge.

Why am I doing this? Because income taxes are complicated. And I've done my best to simplify them for you in this book.

Maybe you'll read this book and say, "Oh, yeah. I understand this stuff! It makes perfect sense." And you'll know exactly what to do to implement the many tax-saving strategies presented here.

It is also possible that you'll read my book and say, "I think I get it. But I sure would like to ask a question or two for clarification, to make sure I understand how to apply a specific tax deduction strategy to my particular situation."

That is the purpose of these Tax Coupons -- to enable you to ask me your questions, and to give you the opportunity to send me your most recently filed income tax returns for my review, to see if you've been overlooking something.

Don't let these coupons just sit here! Use them, and use them right away! Thousands of dollars in tax savings could be waiting for you if you take action and redeem these coupons.

Click here to access the Tax Coupons worth $150 --

www.selfemployedtaxdeductionstoday.com/tax-coupons.pdf

WHY I WROTE THIS BOOK

In 1966 George Harrison wrote a song entitled "Taxman". Perhaps you remember it. My favorite part goes like this:

> "If you drive a car, I'll tax the street,
> If you try to sit, I'll tax your seat.
> If you get too cold I'll tax the heat,
> If you take a walk, I'll tax your feet."

The song ends with these famous words: "I'm the taxman and you're working for no one but me."

Do you ever feel like "you're working for no one" but the taxman? Believe me, you're not alone.

Each year economists do a calculation to determine "Tax Freedom Day" -- a way to graphically depict that as a nation we spend about 30% of our income on taxes. In 2014, Tax Freedom Day was April 21. That means that from January 1 through April 20, all the money you made went to taxes. Finally, on April 21, you now get to keep what you make for the rest of the year! Unbelievable, isn't it?

Source: www.taxfoundation.org

So if you think you are being "nailed" by the government, you are absolutely right. You spend more on taxes than any other category of consumer spending. In fact, you spend more on taxes than on food and housing combined!

Maybe you already knew intuitively that your Tax Bill is outrageously high. If not, the picture I've just painted should thoroughly convince you that you pay too much tax, period.

To put it simply, I wrote this book to lower your taxes. My purpose is to help you pay less tax -- without any fear of an IRS audit.

If you are tired of paying so much in taxes to the government year after year, this book is for you. Here you'll find perfectly legal tax deduction strategies that can reduce your taxes significantly.

Also, please note that this book is written for small business owners and self-employed people. I'll be explaining tax reduction strategies that apply to folks who own a small business or engage in self-employment activities, either full-time or part-time. This also includes solo entrepreneurs, consultants, and those who may work a regular full-time day job but also moonlight on the side with a small business that will hopefully become much bigger some day!

Small business owners include the backbone of our economy – sole proprietors who file a Schedule C with their personal income tax return. It also includes owners of corporations, partnerships and limited liability companies (LLC's). Regardless of the legal entity you happen to have, if you own your own business, this book is for you.

Also included in this book are tax consulting coupons, that if used, can ensure that you and I work together to put these tax-saving strategies to work. Let's get started!

WHAT OTHERS SAY ABOUT THIS BOOK

"This book is clear and concise. It's as simple as tax talk can possibly be." *Terry Rigg*

"This is a goldmine of information. It's worth many times its price, so do yourself a favor and buy it today! I've never seen so much great tax information distilled into simple, even entertaining, explanations. You've never seen taxes like this!" *Julie Wilkinson, author, "My Life at AOL"*

"This book should be required reading for all self-employed business owners. But especially I see this as a highly valuable tool for independent bookkeepers who want to become invaluable to their clients and work in cooperation with CPAs and Enrolled Agents. Reading this book is a great investment
all the way around!" *Gabrielle Fontaine, PB, ASBC TheFreelanceBookkeeper.com*

"I was skeptical too. But Wayne's guarantee that he can save you money on your taxes can't be ignored. And neither can his advice. I say quit giving your money to Uncle Sam and start giving it to Uncle You. You earned it, didn't you? Well, get this and learn how to keep it." *Joe Vitale, www.mrfire.com*

"I thought this stuff would be tricky, hard to follow, or simply something I couldn't find the time to do. Boy, was I ever wrong! Not only do you explain it in easy to understand terms, but you can make it so darned easy to save big time on my taxes. Thanks to your help, I saved $4,600 and I'm going to be able to take a really nice family vacation this year -- all because of your materials, all from the money I normally would have paid on taxes. Thanks for giving me thousands of dollars!" *Grady Smith*

"This book is unlike anything I ever seen. It's written in plain English -- no technical or accounting gobbledygook -- just excellent information you can use immediately. I believe anyone who operates a business online (or offline) can understand the tax saving methods covered here. I personally talked with Wayne for 30 minutes on the phone and absolutely grilled him about how and why a sole proprietor would need this information. His answers not only gave me some tax-saving ideas I never thought of before, but proved to me that this guy really knows his stuff!" *Jim Edwards, www.ebookfire.com*

"Wayne, I just read your book...it's great! Your easy to read and understand tax reduction strategies are excellent. I am going to immediately put your strategy into place to turn personal medical expenses into a legitimate business expense. This strategy alone will save me over $3,500. Keep up the great work!" *Jeffrey Jordan*

"What an eye-opener! I am not a tax person and it usually makes my head spin, but your simple explanations really helped me. It's obvious you really know your loopholes (business). Thanks!" *Livvie Matthews*

"I just read your book and it is fantastic! You've got a knack for taking complicated tax concepts and making them 'un-complicated.' You helped me to understand how easy it is for a small business owner to lower my taxes without spending a lot of time or money." *Michael Senoff*

"Wayne, just wanted to drop you a line and say thanks for sending me thousands of extra dollars in the mail every year! Seriously, I can't believe you are giving this information away at such a low price -- it's a steal. You take all the complexity out of doing my tax return -- I will even ENJOY doing my taxes from now on because I know I'm going to end up with more money in my pocket. Highly recommended, you won't be sorry. *Jeff Smith*

Why You Should **Not** Read This Book

There are three reasons why you should not read this book.

Reason #1

If you're looking for an exhaustive in-depth explanation of every tax deduction under the sun, this book is not for you. There are other books that go into much more detail than this one, and I'll even recommend a couple for you.

Over the years I've come to realize that most self-employed people are incredibly busy. You've got your business to run, and you've got a life outside your business. Or you may have a regular employee-type day job and are moonlighting your self-employment gig on the side, perhaps part-time. You may have two (or more) jobs, along with a family and a house and lots of things going on.

So you probably don't have much time to read and study about tax law. Who does?

This book is written for the self-employed person who wants to get the Big Picture of many of the most important and most beneficial tax deductions available to small biz owners.

I'm trying to take some very complex tax rules and boil them down for you in simple everyday language. I do my best to explain tax laws in Plain English. And I try to do this as concisely as I can. This is a challenge, of course, because our politicians have done a wonderful job making taxes unnecessarily and painfully complicated, convoluted and just plain crazy!

Our tax code and accompanying IRS explanations of the code go on for thousands of pages. It really is sad. So my book is just the tip of the iceberg. But I truly believe that if you read it earnestly, you'll walk away with a good basic understanding of many tax deductions you can start using right away. And if you need more information, check the "Recommended Resources" section at the end of this book.

REASON #2

If you are looking for illegal tax strategies, this book is not for you. Every deduction presented in this book is perfectly legal. If you want to get around the law by breaking the law, I cannot help you.

There are plenty of legal tax reduction strategies. Why monkey around with funny money?

REASON #3

If you have this naive idea that a profitable small business can pay zero taxes, this book is not for you. If your business or self-employment activity is making money, you're going to pay some taxes. And generally speaking, the more money you make, the more taxes you pay.

But it is also very likely that if you are profitable, you can legally reduce your taxes. How much? That all depends on several factors, such as how much profit you're making and what type of entity you have.

The point here is this: don't expect to read this book and then magically have everything you need to know to suddenly pay no taxes at all. That is an unrealistic expectation.

I have had clients who implemented tax strategies explained here and reduced their annual taxes by $2,000 or $3,500 or $6,000.

Will that happen to you? I have no idea. It is possible to lower your taxes by thousands of dollars, but everyone's situation is different and there is no way I can promise you a certain amount of tax savings without knowing all the details of your particular situation.

And also keep in mind that my client who saved $6,000 in taxes was already paying more than $6,000 in small business taxes. And that means he was profitable.

I'm stating the obvious, but it needs to be said: You cannot reduce your taxes by $6,000 unless you already have an annual tax liability of at least $6,000. And you can only have a tax liability of $6,000 if you have taxable income that creates that tax liability.

CHAPTER 1. TAX-SAVING TIP #1 – THE EASIEST WAY TO IMMEDIATELY REDUCE YOUR TAXES

Congratulations! You are the proud owner of one of America's greatest treasures: The Small Business. Without question, our country is truly the "Land of Opportunity." And Small Business Owners like you are the main reason why.

Congratulations on taking the first step to "going it alone." There are probably as many reasons for starting a Small Business as there are people who have started a Small Business. But undoubtedly the most common reason for starting a Small Business is the most obvious one: to make money.

Running a Small Business successfully (and by that, I mean profitably) is a tremendous challenge. There are a multitude of obstacles to making money in your business. And perhaps the most frustrating one that stands in the way of your success is taxes.

We live in a great country, for sure. But our "system" is not without its problems. And one of the greatest problems you face as a Small Business Owners is simply this: "How can I legally reduce my tax bill?"

Taxes: Income Tax, Payroll Tax, Sales Tax, Real Estate Tax, Personal Property Tax, Excise Tax. The seemingly never-ending list of taxes is just that -- a never ending list. It does not end.

And not only is our tax system "never-ending", it is also incredibly frustrating because of its complexity.

Just how complicated is The Tax Code? Consider this: Way back in 1913, when federal income taxes first began, the entire Tax Code occupied a mere half-inch thick book. The first federal income tax return was a simple two-page form with four pages of instructions.

Now what do we have? -- A literal monster! Today the Tax Code takes two four-inch thick volumes to print, along with well over a million lines of "regulations" that officially explain and interpret what the Code means. Then when you add all the relevant tax-related Court decisions that apply the Code -- well, now we're talking about 25 feet of library shelves.

With all these tax regulations, what's the average taxpayer to do? I realize just how intimidating the Tax Code can be to the Small Business owner like yourself. That's why I wrote this book -- to help people like you discover the best ways to legally lower your tax bill.

The first legal loophole is this: Given the same amount of profit, not all businesses pay the same amount of taxes.

Think about that for a moment. It's probably something that you've always wondered about, maybe were even a bit "suspicious" about. Well, if you always thought that some people pay less tax than you (even though they make the same amount of income), you are absolutely correct.

Why is that?

Is it fair?

Is it right?

Is it legal?

Yes, it is absolutely legal for one business owner to pay less tax than another business owner, even though both have the same income.

Why does this happen? I'm going to answer this question by explaining the easiest (and perhaps the most overlooked) tax-reduction strategy on the books. Many small business owners are paying too much tax because they own the wrong type of business.

Now what do I mean by the wrong type of business?

I'm not talking about type in the sense of whether you own a Carpet Cleaning Business vs. a Pet Store. I don't mean what industry your business is in. I don't mean whether you are a manufacturer, a wholesaler, a retailer, or a service business.

Very simply, I'm talking about whether your business is a Sole Proprietorship, a Partnership, a "C" Corporation, an "S" Corporation, or a Limited Liability Company.

There are several types of business ownership, from a legal entity standpoint. And you have got to get this right, or you will pay literally thousands of dollars more in taxes than you should.

I certainly don't want to waste your time going into all the legal pros and cons of how your business should be structured legally. But the simple fact is, there are

17

significant differences in the amount of taxes that each of these business entities usually pay.

And there are probably some very compelling reasons why you picked the type of business structure you currently have. Maybe you have received legal counsel on this matter, and your attorney has told the best way to go from a legal standpoint.

I'd like you to consider the possibility that if your business is a Sole Proprietorship, you could be paying more tax than necessary simply because you are a Sole Proprietorship. And if you would give serious consideration to incorporating your business and choosing to have it taxed as an S Corporation, you could save thousands of dollars in taxes for many years to come.

The next few chapters explain why, so please keep reading.

CHAPTER 2. TAX-SAVING TIP #2 – MAKING THE SWITCH (PART I)

If your business is a Sole Proprietorship, please read this next section carefully. This is probably the most important information about taxes you will ever read.

IMPORTANT: No matter what type of business you own, please read this section. If you are a Partner in a Partnership, or a member/owner of an LLC, or even a corporation shareholder, do not skip this section. It is absolutely critical that you understand the concepts explained here, no matter what type of business you own. In other words, this section is not just for Sole Proprietors. You'll see what I'm talking about after reading this section and the sections that follow.

The reason that Sole Proprietors pay more tax than "S" Corporations is because of something known as Self-Employment Tax. As a Sole Proprietor, you report your business profit on your Personal Income Tax Return via Schedule C (Profit or Loss From Business). Your business profit is added to any other income reported on your personal tax return (from W-2 wages, interest and dividends, or whatever), and is then subject to regular income tax.

But the Sole Proprietor not only pays income tax on his/her business profit. The business profit is also subject to Self-Employment Tax, which is also reported on the Sole Proprietor's personal tax return via Schedule SE (Self-Employment Tax).

This Self-Employment Tax is the equivalent of the Social Security Tax and Medicare Tax (also known as Payroll Taxes) that employees and employers pay on wages. The combined total of Social Security Tax on wages is 12.4% (the employee pays 6.2% and the employer pays 6.2%). The combined total of Medicare Tax on wages is 2.9% (the employee pays 1.45% and the employer pays 1.45%). Altogether, then, a total of 15.3% of employee wages is paid to the government for Payroll Taxes (Social Security and Medicare taxes).

So, if you are an employee, you pay half and your employer pays half. I'm not here to debate whether an employee ever really gets his/her money's worth out of that 7.65%, but at least the employee only has to pay half of the 15.3%.

The Sole Proprietor, on the other hand, has to pay the entire 15.3%.

For purposes of the Self-Employment Tax, the Sole Proprietor is, in effect, treated as both the employer and the employee. I'm sorry to give you the bad news, but that's just the way the system works.

(To be technically correct, the way Schedule SE works, the Sole Proprietor does get a very small break on the 15.3% Self-Employment Tax. For purposes of this discussion -- let's say that the Sole Proprietor ends up paying about 15% Self-Employment Tax on his/her business profit.)

So let's look at an example of a Sole Proprietor's Self-Employment Tax. Let's assume that your business profit, as reported on Schedule C, is $50,000.

Schedule C Profit	$50,000
Self-Employment Tax Rate	x 15%
Self-Employment Tax	$7,500

Now, let's assume that this same business is an "S" Corporation rather than a Sole Proprietorship.

The business has the same $50,000 profit, which is reported on the corporation's income tax return (Form 1120S).

Here's how the "S" Corporation owner ends up paying less tax than the Sole Proprietor.

Let's also assume that the "S" Corporation is run very similarly to the Sole Proprietorship. It's a typical one-person show. The owner does most, if not all of the work.

So, since the business is a Corporation, not a Sole Proprietorship, the business must pay the owner as an employee. In other words, at least some of the $50,000 profit must be paid to the Owner/Employee as wages.

Let's assume, then, that the Fair Market Value of the Owner/Employee's services rendered to the business is about $35,000. In other words, if the "S" Corporation owner went out and hired someone else to do the work, the "S" Corp would have to pay someone $35,000 in wages to do the same work that the owner usually does.

Now here's where the tax savings comes in . . . .

Only the $35,000 in Owner/Shareholder wages would be subject to the 15.3% Payroll Tax.

Of the $50,000 "S" Corporation business profit, only $35,000 is subject to Payroll Taxes. The other $15,000 in profit legally avoids Payroll Tax. If the business is run as a Sole Proprietorship, the entire $50,000 is subject to Self-Employment Tax (the equivalent of Payroll Taxes).

TAKE A LOOK:

"S" Corporation Wages	$35,000
Payroll Tax Rate	x 15%
Payroll Tax	$5,250

Now, let's compare the two scenarios:

SOLE PROPRIETOR: Self-Employment Tax --$7,500

"S" CORPORATION: Payroll Tax --$5,250

TAX SAVINGS FOR THE "S" CORPORATION --$2,250

By simply running your business as "S" Corporation rather than a Sole Proprietorship, you can save $2,250 in taxes. And assuming that you have this kind of profit year after year, you would save $11,250 over 5 years and $22,500 over 10 years.

PLEASE NOTE that this tax savings is NOT a savings in income tax. It is a savings in Payroll Tax (paid by the corporation) vs. Self-Employment Tax (paid by the Sole Proprietorship).

All other things being equal, there is no savings in income tax in the above scenario. Assuming $50,000 of business profit, the Sole Proprietor and the "S" Corporation

Owner/Employee would pay the same amount of income tax, (again, assuming all other things being equal).

So, if you are currently running your business as a Sole Proprietorship, there are some substantial tax savings waiting for you simply by forming an "S" Corporation.

What if you are not a Sole Proprietor? That's OK. There are still substantial tax savings waiting for you . . . .

If you are a Partner in a Partnership, make sure you go on to the next section and read Chapter 3.

If you are a LLC Member in a LLC, make sure you read Chapter 4.

And if you are a Shareholder in a "C" or "S" Corporation, make sure you read Chapter 5 and Chapter 6.

CHAPTER 3. TAX-SAVING TIP #3 – MAKING THE SWITCH (PART II)

If your business is structured as a Partnership, there could be some big tax breaks awaiting you simply by switching over to an "S" Corporation format.

And the reason for this is the same reason given in Chapter 2 -- the "S" Corporation Owner/Employee can pay less in Payroll Taxes than a Partner pays in Self-Employment Taxes.

If you are a Partner in a Partnership but skipped over Chapter 2 because you thought, "Oh, this section is for Sole Proprietorships, not Partnerships", please go back and read Chapter 2.

As a Partnership, you report your partnership business on Form 1065. But this Form 1065 is really just for information purposes. The Partnership usually doesn't pay its own income taxes. Why? Because the Partnership also has to prepare a Schedule K-1 for each Partner, which reports your share of the Partnership's income (or loss). You then take the K-1 information and transfer it to your personal tax return. If your business has a profit, then you pay income tax on that profit via your personal income tax return.

Now, here's the key. Not only do you have to pay income tax on that K-1 profit, you also have to pay Self-Employment tax on that profit. And just like a Sole Proprietor, you have to pay the entire 15.3% Self-Employment Tax on your share of the business profit.

If you switch from a Partnership to an "S" Corporation, you can pay yourself as an employee with some of the business profit, and legally avoid Payroll Taxes on the rest.

Again, this is all explained Chapter 2. The point is simply this -- for Self-Employment Tax purposes, the Partner in a Partnership is treated exactly like the Sole Proprietor. You can legally reduce your Self-Employment Taxes by switching to an "S" Corporation.

CHAPTER 4. TAX-SAVING TIP #4 – MAKING THE SWITCH (PART III)

If your business is structured as an LLC being taxed as a Partnership or Sole Proprietorship, there could be some big tax breaks awaiting you by choosing to be taxed as an "S" Corporation.

And the reason for this is the same reason given in Chapter 2 -- the "S" Corporation Owner/Employee can pay less in Payroll Taxes than a LLC Member pays in Self-Employment Taxes.

If you are an LLC Member but skipped over Chapter 2 because you thought, "Oh, this section is for Sole Proprietorships, not LLC's", please go back to Chapter 2.

As a multi-member LLC being taxed as a Partnership, you must report your LLC business on Form 1065. For multi-member LLC's, this Form 1065 is really just for information purposes. The LLC usually doesn't pay its own income taxes. Why? Because the LLC also has to prepare a Schedule K-1 for each LLC Member, which reports your share of the LLC's income (or loss). You then take the K-1 information and transfer it to your personal tax return. If your business has a profit, then you pay income tax on that profit via your personal income tax return.

Now, here's the key. Not only do you have to pay income tax on that K-1 profit, you also have to pay Self-Employment tax on that profit. And just like a Sole Proprietor, you have to pay the entire 15.3% Self-Employment Tax on your share of the business profit.

If you choose to have your LLC taxed as an "S" Corporation, you can pay yourself as an employee with some of the business profit, and legally avoid Payroll Taxes on the rest.

The same concept applies to a single-member LLC that is being taxed as a Sole Proprietorship because you end up reporting your business on Form 1040, Schedule C and must pay Self-Employment Tax just like a Sole Proprietor.

Again, this is all explained in Chapter 2. The point is simply this -- for Self-Employment Tax purposes, the LLC Member is treated just like the Sole Proprietor. You can legally reduce your Self-Employment Taxes by being taxed as an "S" Corporation.

NOTE: A LLC can choose to be taxed as an S Corporation by filing Form 2553 with the IRS. In other words, the LLC is not required to dissolve the LLC and form a new corporation in order to be taxes as an S Corp.

CHAPTER 5. TAX-SAVING TIP #5 – HOW TO REMOVE THE FEAR OF AN AUDIT

Have you ever been audited by the IRS? Do you know anyone who has been audited by the IRS? There are plenty of "horror stories" out there about IRS auditors swooping down and wreaking havoc on the lives of innocent small business owners.

Believe me, if you've never been audited, you definitely want to keep it that way. Audits are no fun, even if your books are in good shape and you run a clean operation.

Have you ever wondered how the IRS goes about choosing which tax returns to audit? You are about to find out.

Sole proprietorships have a much higher audit rate than corporations. In fact, even sole proprietors with annual sales of less than $25,000 have an audit rate of 2.63%, compared to S Corporations (0.42%) and C Corporations (0.22% for those with annual sales under $250,000).

The audit rate for sole proprietors with sales of $25,000-$99,000 is 1.13%, and sole proprietors with sales greater than $100,000 have an audit rate of 1.36%.

The numbers are very clear: Sole Proprietorships get audited much more than other legal entities of comparable size. Why is that? Because self-employed people are the main reason the U.S. has such a large underground economy, in which millions of dollars of income go unreported every year.

So the IRS has put the most likely suspects at the top of its hit list. You are a Sole Proprietor if you own a business that is unincorporated, i.e. you are not a "C" Corporation or "S" Corporation, nor are you a Partnership or Limited Liability Company (LLC).

The easiest way to know if you are a Sole Proprietorship is to answer this question: Do you report your business on your personal tax return (Form 1040) via Schedule C? If so, you are a Sole Proprietorship, and you are much more likely to get audited than a Corporation, a Partnership, or a Limited Liability Company. This is just a fact of life.

We've already discussed the tax benefits of making the switch from a Sole Proprietorship to a Corporation, especially the "S" Corporation. Now here's another obvious benefit: by being a Corporation, you will dramatically reduce the likelihood of being audited.

The IRS is much more suspicious of Sole Proprietors than Corporations. So it spends more resources going after small business owners who file a Schedule C on their personal tax returns. And Schedule C, as you may already know, tells the IRS all about your business in great detail -- your business income, plus a detailed list of every expense category.

Furthermore, many Sole Proprietors operate their business out of their home office, necessitating another special form known as Form 8829, Expenses for Business Use of Your Home. Well, guess what? Filing Form 8829 also increases the chances for an audit, simply because there's been so much abuse in the area of claiming the Home Office Deduction.

By forming an "S" Corporation, here's what happens:

1. You remove the Schedule C from your personal tax return

2. Instead, your business files a Form 1120S to report its income and expenses. "S" Corporations who file Form 1120S have a much lower audit rate than Sole Proprietors who File Schedule C, as the above chart demonstrates.

3. Since you are running an "S" Corporation, you will receive a Form W-2 for wages earned and a Schedule K-1 for your share of the corporation's profit. Now your personal return is much less likely to get audited. There is no Schedule C, with all its juicy details. Instead, you have a W-2 and a K-1. The W-2 just tells the IRS how much your wages are. The K-1 tells the IRS that you own an "S" Corporation, but typically there is only ONE number that is transferred from the K-1 to the Form 1040. All the details of your business are reported on the Form 1120S. There is no business income or business expense detail on your Form 1040.

4. If you do have a Home Office, you can still deduct those Home Office Expenses on your Form 1120S, but without having to file Form 8829. So you have removed another audit flag from your personal tax return and reported that information on the corporation's tax return, where it is much less likely to be scrutinized, because there is no special IRS form for an "S" Corporation to list Home Office expenses.

5. As a Sole Proprietor, you are supposed to receive a Form 1099-MISC from any individual or business who paid you at least $600 in a calendar year for services rendered. This is

known as non-employee compensation and is reported in Box 7 of Form 1099-MISC. These 1099's are also sent to the IRS, where they are put into the IRS computer and matched up against your Schedule C income. If you don't report this 1099 income, the IRS will know immediately and come knocking on your door.

Once you become an "S" Corporation, you will no longer receive any Forms 1099-MISC. Why? Because the law says corporations don't need to receive Form 1099-MISC. Generally, corporations are excluded from the 1099 rules. So, again, just by being an "S" Corporation, you have taken your business out from under the IRS microscope.

6. The IRS loves to audit Sole Proprietors for two main reasons: First, Sole Proprietors are notorious for under-reporting their income. And second, because Sole Proprietors are notorious for over-stating their expenses, especially in the areas of travel, entertainment, and vehicle expenses. Because you are a Corporation, with a much lower audit rate, chances are pretty good that these typical audit flags will receive less scrutiny.

So there you have it. By switching from a Sole Proprietorship to a Corporation, you will not only save a bundle in taxes, but you will also reduce the risk of audit.

It's hard to assign a dollar value to something like reducing the risk of an audit. But if you've ever been audited before (or know someone who has), you know what a hassle it can be. Many hours spent tracking down receipts and records. Many hours spent fretting and worrying.

Removing this fear and aggravation could well be worth more to you than the tax savings.

IMPORTANT NOTE:

If you've read this far, you realize I'm encouraging you to give serious consideration to the "S" Corporation. For many Small Business Owners and Self-Employed People, it's the way to go.

Whether or not you should form an "S" Corporation, however, depends on several factors: the cost, the additional paperwork, the potential tax savings, your income level, legal and estate planning considerations, among others.

Forming an "S" Corporation is something you should investigate thoroughly before making the switch.

And this is one of the main reasons why I've included the tax consulting coupons in this book. Send me your most recent income tax return and I can tell you the tax consequences of forming an "S" Corporation. And during our 30-minute phone consultation, we can discuss the pros and cons of incorporating for your particular situation.

Yes, many Sole Proprietors are much better off tax-wise by forming an "S" Corporation. But that does not mean that every Sole Proprietor should automatically form an "S" Corporation without first doing some serious research and/or consulting with a tax professional experienced in the area of Choice of Entity.

I am not advocating a "once size fits all" approach to the Choice of Entity issue. The "S" Corporation may be best for you. And it may not.

CHAPTER 6. TAX-SAVING TIP #6 – HOW TO AVOID DOUBLE TAXATION OF CORPORATE PROFITS

If you own a C Corporation, pay attention to this section. One of the first things you should realize is that by owning a C corporation, you have become a victim of one of the most notorious tax bites of all time. What am I talking about? Something known as Double Taxation of Corporate Profits.

Also, if you own a Sole Proprietorship, Partnership, or Limited Liability Company, pay attention to this section. I've already explained one great reason why you should consider an S Corporation (to reduce Payroll Taxes). Now, this section will explain why, assuming you are going to incorporate your business, you should consider forming an S Corporation rather than a C Corporation.

Here's how it works. Let's say you own a C Corporation that makes $10,000 profit in a given year. The C Corporation must then report that $10,000 profit on its corporate income tax return (Form 1120) and pay corporate income tax on that $10,000 profit. C Corporations pay 15% federal income tax on the first $50,000 of profits, so the federal income tax on this $10,000 would be $1,500. (There may be state corporate income tax as well, but for sake of simplicity, let's leave that factor out of this discussion for now.)

So the C Corporation pays the $1,500 federal income tax.

Now, let's say the C Corporation's shareholders (that would be you) want to withdraw that $10,000 profit out of the business. After all, isn't that why the shareholders formed the corporation in the first place -- to make a profit, and to reap the rewards of that profit?

So the corporation pays the $10,000 profit to the shareholders, which is known as a "dividend". Now here's where the notorious tax bite comes into play.

Didn't the corporation already pay federal income tax on that $10,000 profit? Yes. Well, now that the corporation has distributed that $10,000 dividend to the shareholders, the shareholders must report that same $10,000 as taxable income on their personal tax returns.

So that same $10,000 gets taxed twice. Once on the corporation's income tax return, and a second time on the individual shareholders' personal tax returns.

Let's say the shareholders' are in the 15% federal tax bracket. That means the shareholders will pay $1,500 in federal income tax on the $10,000 dividend. This is in addition to the $1,500 of corporate income tax already paid by the corporation. Altogether, that $10,000 of corporate profit resulted in $3,000 in total federal income tax: $1,500 corporate plus $1,500 personal.

Another way to look at it: The $10,000 profit was taxed at a total federal rate of 30% -- 15% corporate tax plus 15% personal tax. Now, if state taxes are factored in, it is very likely that corporate profits are taxed at the rate of 35% - 40%. Ouch.

Think about that: 40% of your business profit is turned over to Uncle Sam. Now you can see why I am so determined to recommend strategies that reduce my clients' tax burden.

Now, how do you legally avoid this Double Taxation of Corporate Profits?

Here's how: By forming an S Corporation.

Why should you form an S Corporation? Here's why:

When you form a corporation, for tax purposes the IRS automatically assumes that you want to be treated as a regular C Corporation, which is subject to the regular rules of corporate taxation as described above. The C Corporation is a stand-alone taxable entity, and must report and pay tax on its profit as a separate legal tax-paying person.

But if you want to avoid double taxation of corporate profits, the corporation files a special form (Form 2553) with the IRS declaring that it wants to be recognized as an S Corporation. The tax code treats an S Corporation differently than a C Corporation. The S Corporation is still a corporation from a legal standpoint, but from a tax standpoint, generally speaking, the S Corporation usually does not have any income tax liability.

Now the S Corporation still files a corporate income tax return (Form 1120S instead of Form 1120), but the S Corporation profits (or losses) are reported on this tax return for information purposes only. Via a special form called Schedule K-1, the "S" Corporation profits (or losses) get transferred from the corporation's tax return to the personal income tax returns of the shareholders. The result is that any corporate profit is only taxed ONCE -- on the personal income tax returns of the individual shareholders.

What does this mean? In the above example, the total federal income tax would be reduced by 15%. The corporation would not pay the 15% federal income tax on Form 1120. Instead, the corporate profit of $10,000 would result in zero corporate income tax. The only income tax paid on this $10,000 would be the 15% personal income tax reported on the shareholder's personal tax returns. Instead of paying tax twice, the corporate profits are subject to tax only once.

Now here's some critical information about how to become an S Corporation. There are specific requirements to becoming an S Corporation. These requirements are listed in detail in the Instructions for Form 2553. Generally speaking, the corporation will probably meet these requirements if all of the following are true:

1. The corporation is a domestic corporation.

2. The corporation has no more than 100 shareholders.

3. The corporation's only shareholders are individuals, estates, certain trusts, or tax-exempt organizations. (If the corporation has a shareholder who is either an estate, trust or a tax-exempt organization, consult a tax professional.)

4. The corporation has no non-resident alien shareholders.

5. The corporation has only one class of stock.

6. The corporation is not one of the following ineligible corporations: certain types of banks, thrift institutions, insurance companies, a "possessions corporation", or a "domestic international sales corporation". (If the corporation falls under one of these categories, consult a tax professional.)

7. The corporation has a regular "calendar year", i.e. the corporation's "tax year" ends on December 31. (If the corporation has a "fiscal year", i.e. a tax year ending on a date other than December 31, consult a tax professional.)

8. Each shareholder consents to the "S" Corporation election.

If your corporation meets the above requirements, great! Now you are ready to file Form 2553, Election by a Small Business Corporation (Under section 1362 of the Internal Revenue Code).

Like many business tax forms, Form 2553 looks worse than it really is. Everything on Page 1 and Page 2 must be completed. Page 3, however, can be disregarded totally by most corporations -- read the fine print to see whether you should complete Page 3.

The most important thing to understand about filing this form is knowing WHEN to file Form 2553. Please read the instructions very carefully, especially the section entitled, When To Make the Election. Unfortunately, these due date instructions are written in typically confusing government-type language. I'll be the first to admit that this is the hardest part of the whole S Corporation process. But it is oh-so-critical that this be done right, or your corporation might not qualify for S Corporation status, even if everything else is OK.

WARNING! If Form 2553 is not filed by the appropriate due date, the election to be treated as an S Corporation will be rejected by the IRS. The result: your corporation will not qualify for S Corporation status and the corporation will have to file the regular C Corporation tax return and be subject to regular corporate income taxes and the dreaded Double Taxation of Corporate Profits discussed earlier.

If the instructions regarding the due date for Form 2553 are not clear to you, please consult a tax professional before filing Form 2553.

Here's an overview of the "due date" instructions for Form 2553:

If you want S Corporation status to take effect for the corporation's first tax year:

1. File Form 2553 within 2 months and 15 days of the beginning of the first tax year. A corporation's first "tax year" begins on the date that the corporation: a) has shareholders b) acquires assets or c) begins doing business (whichever is the first to occur). Often this means that the corporation's first tax year begins on the incorporation date.

EXAMPLE #1: XYZ Corporation begins its first taxable year on June 1, 2014 (the date of incorporation). To be an S Corporation beginning with its first taxable year (2014), XYZ Corporation must file Form 2553 no later than August 15, 2014.

If you want S Corporation status to take effect for a tax year OTHER THAN the corporation's first tax year:

1. File Form 2553 within 2 months and 15 days of the beginning of the current tax year and S Corporation status will take effect for the current tax year.

2. If you want S Corporation status to take effect January 1 of the following tax year, file Form 2553 at any time during the previous tax year.

What if you missed either of the "2 month and 15 day" deadlines as explained above?

Do not despair! There are special rules that may allow the corporation to still qualify for S Corporation status even though the Form 2553 was not filed on time. There are specific conditions that must be met which are beyond the scope of this book.

If you missed either of the "2 month and 15 day" deadlines, consult a tax professional.

In conclusion:

Are you still with me? Like I said before, these Form 2553 due date instructions are both confusing and critical. Do not hesitate to contact a tax professional to make sure your corporation submits Form 2553 on time. Being an S Corporation can result in significant tax savings -- don't miss out on these tax savings because you filed Form 2553 late.

CHAPTER 7. TAX-SAVING TIP #7 – PAY YOURSELF THE RIGHT AMOUNT OF COMPENSATION

Now that I've explained why the "S" Corporation is often the best type of business to own from a tax-saving standpoint, let's talk a little more about this issue of compensation.

Many times a new business will go through the following sequence of events:

A business is started, usually as a sole proprietorship or informal partnership. After a year or two of at least break-even or even mildly profitable success, the business decides to incorporate. During this initial period before incorporation, the business did not have to worry about payroll. Sole proprietorships and partnerships simply distribute the profits to the owners; technically, these distributions of profit are not wages or salary to the owners. And there are no payroll tax returns or W-2's to file (unless, of course, the business had any non-owner employees).

After incorporation, however, things are different. Now, if a shareholder performs services for the corporation, the corporation must pay the shareholder as an employee. And in a small, one-person or family-run business, it is very likely that all shareholders are actively involved in the day-to-day operation of the business, providing services to the corporation that must be compensated with wages or salary.

So even if there are no non-shareholder employees, a corporation with just one shareholder also has just one employee -- the sole shareholder is both owner and employee of the corporation. And having just one employee (even if it is the shareholder-employee) results in the necessity of filing all federal, state and local payroll tax returns.

At the federal level, this means filing the following payroll tax returns: Form 941 (quarterly), Form 940 (annually), Form W-2 (annually), and Form W-3 (annually). In addition, federal payroll tax payments are usually due each month via the electronic federal tax payment system (EFTPS).

At the state and local level, this means filing any number of additional payroll tax returns, depending on what state the corporation is in. In Indiana, for example, having just one employee means filing Form WH-1 (monthly or quarterly), Form UC-1 (quarterly), and state copies of Form W-2 (annually) and Form WH-3 (annually).

So an Indiana corporation with just one shareholder-employee faces a literal mountain of payroll-related paperwork. Altogether, being an employer in Indiana with just one employee results in the filing of some 37 payroll tax returns during the course of one year. Other states have similar payroll reporting requirements. Amazing but true!

Of course, knowing which payroll tax returns to file and when to file them is no small matter. Some are due monthly, some quarterly, some annually. If you are confused about payroll tax returns, please consult a tax professional! You do not want to get behind in this area. Many small businesses fail simply because of the failure to file payroll tax returns and/or the failure to pay payroll taxes.

Another area of confusion for many corporation owners has to do with how much compensation to pay the shareholder-employee(s). It is common for corporation owners to assume that all profit should be distributed to the shareholder-employee(s) as salary or wages, regardless of what services were done by the shareholder-employee. In the case of a "C" Corporation, this strategy is often viewed as "appropriate" because it ensures that no profit will be left in the company, subject to double taxation. And there very well may be situations when this is the best approach.

But with an "S" Corporation, it may be appropriate to pay salary/wages to the shareholder-employee(s) which are less than the available profit. Here's an example to illustrate this concept:

XYZ Corp has profit of $60,000 in a given tax year (before shareholder-employee salary/wages are deducted). XYZ has one shareholder-employee who owns 100% of the stock. This shareholder-employee also works full-time for the corporation, providing services which have a fair market value of $40,000. By paying the shareholder-employee $40,000 of salary/wages instead of $60,000 (the available profit), the corporation and the shareholder-employee save about $3,060 in Social Security and Medicare taxes ($20,000 x 15.3%).

Think about this. Here's an incredibly simple-to-understand and easy-to-implement tax-saving strategy. Just by paying yourself $40,000 wages instead of $60,000 wages, you save yourself about $3,000.

The key concept here is: What is the fair market value (FMV) of the shareholder-employee's services? It is critical that the corporation pay reasonable compensation for any employee's services, including services provided by the shareholder-employee(s). In the above example, if the shareholder-employee provided services that could have been obtained in the public labor market for $40,000, then that is what the corporation should pay the shareholder-employee. In other words, if the corporation could have hired someone other than the shareholder-employee to do the same job for $40,000, then $40,000 can be documented as reasonable compensation. Why pay more than FMV for an employee's services?

In other words, just because the corporation has $60,000 in profit does NOT necessarily mean that the corporation has to pay out the entire $60,000 as wages to the shareholder/employee. If the shareholder/employee's work is not worth $60,000, then it is foolish to pay the entire $60,000 as wages.

Now, you may be wondering, "What about the other $20,000 of profit? How do I pay myself the rest of the profit?" Good question! The answer is simply this: The $20,000 remaining profit can be paid to the shareholder/employee as a distribution of profit. The corporation just pays the $20,000 to the shareholder whenever the corporation deems it appropriate to do so. This $20,000 of profit distribution is NOT treated as a paycheck -- this $20,000 is not wages or salary or a bonus for work done as an employee. Rather, it is simply the payment of profit to the corporation's owner. And because it is a distribution and not a paycheck, there are no payroll taxes withheld from the distribution -- no Social Security tax, no Medicare tax, no federal unemployment tax, and no state unemployment tax.

If you are the owner of an "S" Corporation who happens to also work for the "S" Corporation as an employee, think of yourself as wearing two hats -- one hat is labeled Shareholder, the other hat is labeled Employee. When you put on your Employee Hat, you get paid wages (or salary) for the services you perform, based on the Fair Market Value of the work you did, just like you'd pay any other employee in a true arm's length business transaction.

When you put on your Shareholder Hat, you get paid Distributions for being the owner of the business who is entitled to receive his/her share of the corporation's profits. These distribution payments are not payments for services rendered, but rather are your reward for starting the business, investing capital in the business, and assuming the risk of owning the business.

Another common question you may have is, "Well, how does all this get reported on my personal income tax return?"

With an "S" Corporation, the $40,000 salary/wages will be reported on the shareholder's personal income tax return via the From W-2. The corporation will then have a profit of $20,000 which will also be reported as income on the shareholder's personal income tax return via the Schedule K-1. So whether the corporation pays salary/wages of $40,000 or $60,000 will have no effect on the shareholder's personal income tax liability. But by reporting only $40,000 of wages instead of $60,000, the corporation and the shareholder will realize a substantial savings in payroll taxes.

This area of shareholder-employee "reasonable compensation" is critical. The corporation should not pay too much salary/wages and end up paying too much payroll tax. On the other hand, the corporation must be careful to not underpay the shareholder-employee. If the shareholder-employee performs services to the corporation, this should result in payment of reasonable compensation. To not pay the shareholder-employee any salary/wages will likely raise a red flag with the IRS. And paying the shareholder-employee less than FMV for services rendered is also likely to draw attention from the IRS. Do not fail to pay close attention to this area.

So I must end this section with a strong warning:

If you perform employee-type work for the corporation, do not think you can get away with paying yourself zero wages and all distributions.

This trick has been tried and it does not work. The IRS will look closely at the tax return of an "S" Corporation that reports zero wages to its officers and/or shareholders. In a small, family-run "S" Corporation, the shareholders, officers and employees are often the same people. In fact, if you convert a Sole Proprietorship to an "S" Corporation (which I think is a great idea and could save you thousands of dollars in taxes), it is very likely that there is just one person who is sole shareholder, the only officer, and the one and only employee.

Assuming the Corporation is profitable, this one shareholder/employee must be paid something as an employee. To pay no wages and all distributions is a big mistake! A few unscrupulous "S" Corporation owners have tried to get away with it, and were caught red-handed. The IRS simply said, "Since the owner also performed work for the corporation as an employee, some/most/all of those distributions must be re-classified as wages, and the appropriate payroll taxes must be paid on those wages."

So the whole point behind this chapter is not to get away with paying no payroll taxes. Rather, the point here is to legally reduce the amount of payroll taxes you pay, possibly by thousands of dollars each year.

Chapter 8. Tax-Saving Tip #8 – How To Deduct Losses Now Rather Than Later

Tax-Saving Tip #8 is yet another reason why many small business owners prefer the "S" Corporation over the "C" Corporation. The following comments regarding deductibility of "S" Corporation losses will usually apply to Partnership and LLC losses, too.

Many small businesses lose money during their early years. This is a fact of life. I wish this were not the case, but it is. So let's just be honest about it. You may be able to generate a profit right from the start, and if so, congratulations!

But for those businesses that are not profitable, there is some consolation: corporations are allowed to deduct losses against income, thereby saving taxes. But *when* a corporation gets to deduct those losses, and *how* a corporation gets to deduct those losses depends on what type of corporation you own.

From a "loss deduction" standpoint, the tax code treats "C" Corporations and "S" Corporations very differently. "C" Corporations, which are treated as stand-alone taxable entities, can only deduct one year's loss against another year's profit. This is known as the "carryback" or "carryforward" rule of loss deduction. Usually, a net operating loss may be "carried back" 2 years or "carried forward" 20 years. If you have a loss in your first year, there are no previous years to "carryback" the loss, so you can only "carryforward" the loss to the first year when you have a profit. Assuming you eventually have a profit in a future year, the loss will eventually be deductible, resulting in a tax benefit. But you have to wait until you have a profit to deduct the loss.

With an "S" Corporation, there is a different set of rules altogether. Generally speaking, an "S" Corporation does not pay income tax on net profit from business activity. Instead, "S" Corporations pass through profits and losses to the shareholders, who report those profits and losses on their personal tax returns.

So, if your "S" Corporation has a loss in the first year, the shareholders can usually report that loss on their personal tax returns, using that loss to offset other income and thereby reducing their personal income tax in the year of the "S" Corporation loss. There is no waiting until the "S" Corporation has a profit.

This deductibility of "S" Corporation losses on shareholder tax returns can be a major benefit of choosing "S" Corporation status. Consider the following example.

Mr. Taxpayer forms an XYZ Corporation as an "S" Corporation on January 1st. Mr. Taxpayer owns 100% of the stock of XYZ Corporation. The corporation suffers a $5,000 loss in its first year. Mr. Taxpayer's wife, Mrs. Taxpayer, works a regular full-time job and earns salary of $95,000 as reported on her W-2. Mr. & Mrs. Taxpayer are in the 25% federal tax bracket. Mr. Taxpayer is allowed to report the $5,000 loss on his personal tax return; therefore the $5,000 "S" Corp loss offsets a portion of Mrs. Taxpayer's income, resulting in a federal tax savings of $1,250 ($5,000 x 25%).

Assuming Mr. and Mrs. Taxpayer also pay state income tax of 5%, they will realize an additional savings of $250 ($5,000 x 5%).

So, because Mr. Taxpayer formed an "S" Corporation, he saves a total of $1,500 in federal and state income taxes.

Compare this to what would have happened if XYZ Corporation had been a "C" Corporation. First of all, Mr. and Mrs. Taxpayer would have paid $1,500 more income tax in Year One of the corporation. The $5,000 loss would have been "carried forward" to Year Two, when it could have been deducted against the first $5,000 of profit earned in that year. If there was a loss in Year Two, the Year One loss and the Year Two loss would have been "carried forward" to Year Three and so on, until the corporation made a profit.

Which would you rather do -- save taxes now or save taxes later? In most cases, it is usually better to reduce taxes now, especially when you consider the time value of money.

CHAPTER 9. TAX-SAVING TIP #9 – HOW TO PAY YOURSELF FIRST (AND GET THE GOVERNMENT TO CHIP IN)

The SIMPLE Plan described below is available to virtually all types of business entities: Corporations (both "C" and "S"), Partnerships, LLC's, and Sole Proprietorships. So from a "business entity" standpoint, there is no good reason not to have a SIMPLE Plan.

Every now and then, Congress and the President pass legislation that is actually beneficial to taxpayers, including small business owners like yourself. The Small Business Job Protection Act of 1996, which became law August 20, 1996, created a simplified retirement plan for small businesses. This new type of retirement plan was available on January 1, 1997 and is called the "Savings Incentive Match Plan for Employees" -- or the SIMPLE Plan. And believe it or not, compared to other types of employer-sponsored retirement plans, the SIMPLE Plan is truly simple. It is simple to understand, simple to implement, and simple to maintain.

As a small business owner, you may already have employees. If you don't currently have employees, you probably will have to consider hiring employees if you want your business to grow.

If you are the corporation's only employee (or if you are a Sole Proprietor, Partner, or LLC member), or if your only other employees are family members, the SIMPLE Plan is still a great tax-saving strategy. Even with just one employee (you), you can take advantage of the benefits of saving for retirement and paying less tax at the same time.

Of course having employees means offering benefits to obtain and retain those employees. Today, having an attractive retirement plan can play a big role in recruiting and keeping valued employees. But many small business owners may not be able to offer a plan like the popular 401(k) plan, given its high administrative and recordkeeping costs. Simply put, a 401(k) plan is expensive, costing hundreds or even thousands of dollars each year just for administrative tasks which are typically handled by a third-party retirement plan administrator.

This is where the SIMPLE Plan comes to your rescue. It is the ideal low-cost, low-maintenance alternative to the 401(k) plan. The SIMPLE Plan offers many 401(k) plan-like features (such as employee tax-deductible contributions and employer matching contributions) at a much lower cost. Under the SIMPLE Plan, employees make tax-deductible contributions to a SIMPLE IRA maintained by the employer. The employer also makes matching contributions to this same SIMPLE IRA account. Here's how the SIMPLE Plan works:

ELIGIBILITY REQUIREMENTS FOR EMPLOYERS

You can offer a SIMPLE Plan if you:

1. Employ 100 or fewer employees

2. Do not concurrently maintain any other employer-sponsored retirement plan

ELIGIBILITY REQUIREMENTS FOR EMPLOYEES

Your employees are eligible to participate if they:

1. Earned at least $5,000 in any two preceding years, and

2. Expect to earn at least $5,000 during the current year.

Important: You can make the employee eligibility requirements less restrictive or even eliminate them entirely. So, you can reduce the $5,000 compensation requirement to any amount you wish, or not have any compensation requirement at all. This offers you much flexibility. For example, if you want to exclude part-time employees from participation, you would keep the $5,000 requirement. If you want to include as many employees as possible, even those that make only a few hundred dollars a year, than you would eliminate the compensation requirement completely.

EMPLOYEE CONTRIBUTIONS

In 2014, if younger than 50, eligible employees can contribute up to $12,000 of his or her compensation to the SIMPLE-IRA. If age 50 or older, the maximum contribution is $14,500. The employee's contribution is tax-deductible, just like a 401(k) plan or a "traditional" IRA.

These employee contributions can only be made via payroll deduction. The employer must submit the employee's payroll deductions to the SIMPLE-IRA account no later than 30 days after the end of the month in which the contribution was deducted from compensation.

EMPLOYER MATCHING CONTRIBUTIONS

The employer is required to make contributions to each participant's SIMPLE-IRA. Each year, the employer may select one of the following two methods:

1. A dollar-for-dollar match of participating employee contributions, up to 3% of compensation. This match can be decreased to as low as 1% for two years out of five.

Each of the following examples assumes the employer chooses to match up to 3% of each participating employee's compensation:

Example #1: Employee A makes $10,000 and contributes 10% ($1,000) to his SIMPLE-IRA. The employer is required to contribute 3% of the employee's compensation, or $300.

Example #2: Employee B makes $10,000 and contributes 60% ($6,000) to her SIMPLE-IRA. The employer is required to contribute 3% of the employee's compensation, or $300.

Example #3: Employee C makes $10,000 and contributes 1% ($100) to his SIMPLE-IRA. The employer is required to contribute 1% of the employee's compensation, or $100.

Example #4: Employee D makes $10,000 and chooses not to participate, contributing zero to her SIMPLE-IRA. The employer's matching contribution is therefore zero.

The critical factor here: Only those employees who participate by making their own contributions will receive the employer match. If an employee chooses not to contribute to his/her SIMPLE-IRA, then the employee receives no employer match.

2. A flat 2% contribution of all eligible employees' compensation.

The critical factor here: All eligible employees receive the 2% employer contribution, including any employees who did not participate by making their own contributions.

BENEFITS FOR EMPLOYEES

(including Corporate Shareholder-Employees, Partnership Partners, LLC Members & Sole Proprietors)

1. All contributions are tax-deductible. This reduces your current income tax bill.

2. The employee's maximum annual contribution is currently $12,000 (or $14,500 if 50 or older) -- which is significantly more than the annual limit of $5,500/$6,600 for IRA's.

3. Like 401(k) and IRA accounts, all contributions and earnings grow tax deferred until withdrawn. Earnings can compound faster than they would in a comparable taxable investment because they're not being eroded each year by taxes.

4. Contributions are made automatically via payroll deduction. This is probably the most convenient way to save money for retirement. The employee never sees the

money -- it goes right into the SIMPLE-IRA account. What an easy way to save!

5. Both employee and employer contributions are immediately 100% vested.

6. The employer contributions are mandatory. Employees are rewarded with a great tax-free benefit.

7. The employer contributions provide an extra incentive for the employee to participate.

If the employer is using the matching method to determine the employer's contribution, the employee must contribute in order to receive the employer contribution.

8. Virtually all employees will be able to participate, regardless of income level, because many SIMPLE Plan sponsors (such as mutual fund companies) will accept monthly employee contributions of as little as $25.

BENEFITS FOR EMPLOYERS

1. You are providing a tremendous fringe benefit to your employees. This will help you to attract and retain quality employees.

2. All employer contributions are tax-deductible.

3. You are not locked in to only one employer contribution method. There is flexibility here -- you may choose the contribution method that best suits your needs, and you may change the contribution method each year. Under the matching method, you even have the option of reducing the

match to as low as 1% for any two years out of a five-year period.

4. If you use the matching method of employer contribution, only participating employees receive a match. If no employees participate, you are not required to make a matching contribution.

5. The administrative responsibilities are very minimal. There are no burdensome discrimination tests (which do exist for 401(k) plans and other types of employer-sponsored retirement plans). And there are no complicated IRS annual reports, which are required for 401(k) plans and pension plans.

6. The administrative cost is practically zero. Many SIMPLE Plan sponsors (such as mutual fund companies) charge a minimal set-up fee of as little as $100. Plan sponsors rarely charge the employer any further ongoing annual fees. Employees are typically charged a nominal annual SIMPLE-IRA trustee fee of $15 or $20.

7. By providing a retirement plan to your employees, you are encouraging your employees to share the responsibility of funding their own retirement. It is hard for many people to save any money at all -- having some "help" from their employer may be the only retirement planning help your employees ever receive.

The SIMPLE Plan provides numerous benefits for both the employer and employee. Whether you are a one-person business or a small business with up to 100 employees, the SIMPLE Plan offers many nice perks.

HOW TO ESTABLISH A SIMPLE PLAN

There are some specific requirements regarding the implementation of a SIMPLE Plan which are beyond the scope of this book. Be sure to consult a tax or investment professional to make sure you follow these rules properly. Setting up a SIMPLE Plan is not difficult or time-consuming, but a few forms must be completed, including Form 5304-SIMPLE.

A SIMPLE Plan is both a "tax vehicle" and an "investment vehicle." The employer sends in the money (both employee and employer contributions) to each employee's SIMPLE-IRA account. There are many investment options available for a SIMPLE-IRA, so you must consult with a financial institution which offers SIMPLE-IRA accounts.

CHAPTER 10. TAX-SAVING TIP #10 – PAYING YOURSELF FIRST KEEPS GETTING BETTER

Over the years the government has changed the rules regarding SIMPLE Plans. From 1997 through 2000, the maximum employee contribution was $6,000 per year. In 2001, the maximum employee contribution was $6,500 per year. And don't forget, for purposes of the SIMPLE Plan, an employee includes Sole Proprietors, Partners, and LLC Members, plus Corporation Shareholders who also work as an employee for the Corporation they own.

Since 2002, the maximum amount that each employee can contribute to a SIMPLE Plan per year has continued to increase and for 2014 is $12,000 for those under 50 and $14,500 for those 50 and older.

If you operate a profitable business and are looking for a way to both reduce your taxes now and put aside substantial amounts of money for later, this is a fantastic opportunity for the Small Business Owner.

The current SIMPLE Plan limit of $12,000/$14,500 is comparable to the amounts that employees of large companies have been able to put into other more expensive retirement plans such as 401(k)s and 403(b)s. Finally, the government has done something good (for a change) for the Small Business Owner. Take advantage of it!

If your business is just starting out, or you've been struggling lately just to break even, perhaps you're not in a position yet to save this kind of money for retirement. But at least now you are aware of what you can do for yourself once your business becomes profitable and you can afford to pay yourself first.

Think about this: How many bills do you pay each month? How many other people get your money? Too many to count? Probably. You deserve to pay yourself something each year -- something that continues to grow until you are ready to retire. Only you can start saving today.

CHAPTER 11. TAX-SAVING TIP #11 – HOW TO DEDUCT ALL YOUR MEDICAL EXPENSES

The Medical Reimbursement Plan (MRP) described below works best for "C" Corporations and Sole Proprietorships. "S" Corporations and Partnerships can also have a MRP, but the tax benefits are not as great.

One of the most misunderstood aspects of tax law concerns the deductibility of medical expenses. Many people may have a vague idea that medical expenses are deductible on their personal income tax returns, but over the years I have become acutely aware that most people are just plain clueless about this.

Yes, medical expenses are potentially deductible on your personal income tax return, provided you meet both of the following two conditions:

1. You itemize deductions on Schedule A.

So if you take the standard deduction, forget about deducting any medical expenses. And remember, it is only advantageous to itemize deductions if your total itemized deductions exceed your standard deduction.

2. Your medical deductions exceed 10% of your Adjusted Gross Income (AGI)

Adjusted Gross Income is simply your gross income less any adjustments like a deductible IRA contribution. As an example, let's say your AGI is $50,000. Multiply $50,000 times 10% to get the magic number of $5,000. You can deduct medical expenses only to the extent that your medical expenses exceed $5,000. In other words, your first $5,000 of medical expenses is not deductible. If you have $6,000 of medical expenses, the first $5,000 ($50,000 x 10%) is non-deductible; only $1,000 is deductible.

So you can see how tough it is to deduct medical expenses on your personal income tax return. The large majority of taxpayers are not eligible to take this deduction, and now that you understand how the rule works, it is easy to understand why.

Of course, many people are covered by an employer-sponsored health insurance plan, and often these plans provide excellent coverage at affordable group rates. So employees of large companies may not have to worry too much about medical expenses. There may be a deductible and co-insurance payments, so out-of-pocket medical costs may only be a few hundred dollars per year. And if a more major medical problem occurs, like a serious illness or accident, often a very high percentage (say 80% or 90%) of the employee's medical cost is covered.

But what about the small business owner like yourself. Now that you have formed your own business, you may not have an employer-sponsored health insurance plan to rely on. Small business owners frequently must purchase health insurance on their own, and often must pay much higher insurance premiums than a large company gets on a group plan. And an individually purchased plan may not provide the same level of benefits -- resulting in higher deductibles, higher co-payments, and more out-of-pocket expenditures.

Well, there is a way for the small business owner to save taxes by deducting 100% of his/her medical expenses, including health insurance premiums. This strategy is known as a Medical Reimbursement Plan (MRP). The MRP utilizes IRS Code Section 105, which allows small business owners to deduct 100% of their insurance premiums and out-of-pocket medical expenses not covered by insurance.

Let's use the above example: You have $6,000 of medical expenses. Assuming you have $50,000 of AGI and are able itemize deductions on your personal income tax return, only $1,000 of these medical expenses are deductible. If you are in the 15% federal income tax bracket, this will reduce your taxes by only $150 ($1,000 x 15%).

Instead, your business establishes a Section 105 Medical Reimbursement Plan. Let's also assume that you are the business' only employee. So now you simply submit documentation of your medical expenses to your business (which is you), and the business reimburses you the $6,000. Now the full $6,000 of medical expenses is fully deductible by the business as a legitimate business expense. Assuming the business is in the 15% tax bracket, this results in an income tax savings of $900 rather than $150.

To make this arrangement even better, there are payroll tax savings as well. These reimbursed medical expenses (in the above example -- $6,000) are not considered taxable compensation (i.e. wages or salary) to the shareholder/employee. Had this $6,000 been paid to the shareholder/employee as wages/salary, the business and the employee would have paid of total of 15.3% in social security/medicare payroll taxes (7.65% paid by the business plus 7.65% paid the employee). So, $918 in payroll taxes was saved by paying this $6,000 as a tax-free fringe benefit rather than as taxable compensation.

Of course, the higher your medical expenses, the higher your tax savings. And don't forget that the MRP can reimburse you for both health insurance premiums and out-of-pocket medical expenses not covered by insurance.

To create the MRP requires some careful planning and formal paperwork. Here's an overview of what to do.

STEP ONE: Formal adoption of the Medical Reimbursement Plan

The business must formally adopt a Section 105 Medical Reimbursement Plan, subject to the non-discrimination rules and regulations established by the Department of Labor. This means that you must offer the MRP to all employees who meet eligibility requirements, including any non-family employees.

A word of caution is in order here: If you have non-family employees who meet the eligibility requirements, you may not want to establish the MRP. It may be too expensive to pay all eligible employee medical expenses.

The most common situation for effective utilization of the MRP is a "one-person" corporation or a family-owned corporation in which all employees are family members. The most common example is a corporation which is 100% owned by one person, and that one person is the only employee of the corporation. Another good example would be a corporation with just a few family-member shareholders, and the only employees are the shareholders and immediate family-members of the shareholders. Then the corporation's liability to reimburse employee medical expenses is limited to the family members who own the corporation.

Another common scenario for the MRP to work well involves a Sole Proprietorship in which one spouse is the Owner of the business and the other spouse is an employee of the business.

This concept of limited exposure is critical because the MRP must comply with the non-discrimination rules and regulations of the Department of Labor. You, the employer, must establish the eligibility requirements that your employees must meet to participate in the plan. The following list of eligibility requirements show the maximum requirement allowed:

1. Hours -- Any employee working at least 25 hours/week must be included in the plan

2. Seasonal Employees -- Any employee that works at least seven months/year must be included in the plan

3. Age -- any employee over age 25 must be included in the plan

4. Current Employees -- Any current employee who has worked for you more than 36 months must be included in the plan

5. New Employee -- Any future employee who completes 36 months of service for you must be included in the plan.

A few comments about the about list of eligibility requirements:

You may select any of these requirements up to the maximum allowed, but you are also permitted to select a lower requirement for participation. For example, if you choose to exclude employees based upon the number of hours worked, you may choose to exclude employees who do not complete 20 hours of work per week, even though the maximum exclusion is 25 hours per week. This would exclude any employee who works less than 20 hours/week, and would include any employee that works at least 20 hours/week.

The ability to select a lower requirement applies to any of the regulations for participation in the MRP.

Any of the regulations listed above may exclude an employee from participating in the MRP.

IMPORTANT: If you choose not to select any eligibility requirements, all employees will be eligible for participation.

So, if you have non-family employees and you want to limit your reimbursement exposure, study these eligibility requirements closely. It may be possible to still hire non-family employees and legally exclude them from the MRP, provided you follow these MRP setup rules carefully. For example, you could utilize the 25 hour/week requirement to legally exclude all part-time employees. Maybe your business can be run with non-family employees only working part-time (25 hours/week or less). The only full-time employees (more than 25 hours/week) would be family-member employees.

This step of formal adoption of the MRP is critical. Plan documents must be created that meet the above-mentioned non-discrimination rules and regulations established by the Department of Labor. Do not treat this step lightly. If you think that your business is a candidate for a MRP, please consult a tax professional.

STEP TWO: Implementation of the Medical Reimbursement Plan

Here's where common sense and good record-keeping come in to play. If this is a real Medical Reimbursement Plan, then the employee must submit documentation to the business of the employee's medical expenses, and the business must reimburse the employee for those expenses. In other words, the employee must provide receipts for the expenses and the business must then pay the employee for the expenses with a check from the business checking account. It is critical that these simple paperwork procedures be followed. Do not treat the reimbursement procedure casually.

CHAPTER 12. TAX-SAVING TIP #12 – KEEP IT ALL IN THE FAMILY

Legal Loophole #12 can apply to all types of business entities: Corporations (both "C" and "S"), Partnerships, and Sole Proprietorships.

Yes, it is perfectly legal to put your child on the payroll. This is a great tax-saving strategy for many family-owned and family-operated small businesses.

First things first, however. Be careful to pay close attention to the following guidelines:

1. The child must actually perform the work for which he/she is paid.

2. The compensation must be reasonable.

3. The work done by the child must be necessary for the business. In other words, if your child did not do the work for which they were paid, the business would have had to hire someone else to do it.

These guidelines are merely common sense. Simply put, your child must be treated like any other bona fide employee.

Now, here's why this strategy can save you significant tax dollars:

1. A child who can be claimed as a dependent on your personal tax return is still entitled to claim a standard deduction on his/her own personal tax return. For 2014,

the standard deduction for a dependent child can be as much as $6,100.

So, a child employed by his parent's business could earn up to $6,100 of wages income tax-free.

2. The child's wage expense is a legitimate business expense, fully deductible on the parent's business tax return.

The end result: Within the family, up to $6,100 has been paid by the business to the child. The business deducts the wage expense, thereby reducing the business' profit. The child receives a W-2 and reports the wages on his/her personal tax return, but if the wage amount is $6,100 or less, the child will pay no income tax on this earned income.

Should the child receive more than $6,100 of wages, there is still significant tax savings. The first $6,100 is tax-free income. All wages above $6,100 will be taxed at the child's income tax rate (probably 10% for federal tax purposes), which is likely to be much lower than the parent's income tax rate. For example, if the parent is in the 28% tax bracket, the family unit has saved 18% (28% - 10%) of the wage amount over $6,100.

3. If the child is age 17 or younger and your business is a Sole Proprietorship, a single-member LLC, or a husband-wife partnership, here's another great tax benefit to hiring your child: the child's wages are not subject to Social Security and Medicare taxes.

This is another great loophole that can put thousands in your pocket every year.

Have real businesses actually implemented this strategy successfully? You bet! Here's an example, taken from Tax Court records:

The Facts:

The taxpayers owned a mobile-home park and hired their three children, aged 7, 11, and 12 to work there. The children cleaned the grounds, did landscaping work, maintained the swimming pool, answered phones, and did minor repair work. The taxpayers deducted $17,000 of wages paid to the children over a three-year period. But the IRS objected and the case went to trial.

Court's Decision:

Over $15,000 of wage deductions were approved. Most of the deductions that were disallowed were attributable to the 7-year old. But even $1,200 of his earnings was approved by the Court.

So, this strategy has been effectively used, in spite attempts by the IRS to disallow such child employee wages. If you have children who can perform tasks essential to the operation of your business, give this strategy serious consideration.

CHAPTER 13. TAX-SAVING TIP #13 – FORGET ABOUT DEPRECIATION

Tax-Saving Tip #13 can apply to all types of business entities: Corporations (both "C" and "S"), Partnerships, and Sole Proprietorships.

Depreciation expense is one of the most complex and convoluted areas of tax law. Over the years, lawmakers have seemingly gone out of their way to unnecessarily complicate a very routine business practice: how to deduct the cost of business property.

For the typical small business owner, the concept of depreciation can seem very foreign at first. (Have you ever looked at these depreciation rules? I mean, we are talking about some really wacky stuff. When I say that depreciation is a foreign concept for the average small business owner to grasp, I mean really foreign -- like you might as well be reading Greek.)

Many other expenses, like telephone expense, utilities expense, office supplies, salary and wages, are simply deductible in the year in which the expense was incurred. If you pay for something business-related, you normally get to deduct that cost immediately.

One of the major exceptions to the above-mentioned general rule concerns depreciable property, which is defined as property which meets the following basic requirements:

The property must be used in business or held to produce income.

The property must have a determinable useful life longer than one year.

The property must be something that wears out, decays, gets used up, becomes obsolete, or loses its value from natural causes.

The most common types of depreciable property for small business owners include office furniture, office equipment, machinery, vehicles, and buildings.

Now here's where things start to get complicated. If you buy a piece of property for use in your business, like a computer or a printer, this item is not treated like office supplies or the electric bill. Just because you paid for it in 2014 (or any other year) doesn't mean you get to deduct the purchase price in 2014. Instead, you have to deduct the purchase price over a certain number of years, depending on what asset class the item belongs to. It could be 3 years, 5 years, 7 years, 10 years, 15 years, 20 years, and for real estate, as much as 27.5 years or 39 years. The tax law has classified just about every conceivable type of depreciable property into so many categories that it boggles the mind.

And there is a literal boatload of obscure rules regarding different ways to calculate what percentage of the purchase price gets deducted each year over the 3-year period or 5-year period, or whatever time period applies. There are several acceptable methods, each with their own peculiarly stupid rules and exceptions to rules. It's quite a system!

But enough of my droning on and on about these insane depreciation rules. For most small business owners there is a way out of this mess. Fortunately, the government had enough sense to pass legislation that provides a significant exception to all these deprecation rules. This exception is known as the Section 179 Deduction and if you apply the provisions of Section 179, you will probably be able to fully deduct most, if not all, of your business equipment costs in the year of purchase, rather than having to wait any number of years to write off the cost.

Of course, there are rules regarding what types of property can and cannot be deducted under Section 179, and there are also rules regarding how much property can be deducted under Section 179. Do not despair. I'll give you the most important features of Section 179 that most likely apply to you, the small business owner.

WHAT TYPES OF PROPERTY CAN BE DEDUCTED UNDER SECTION 179?

Generally, tangible personal property can be 100% deducted in the year of purchase rather than depreciated over several years. Tangible personal property includes many commonly purchased items for use in a small business: office equipment (including computers, monitors, printers, scanners), office furniture, machinery, and tools.

The major category of property that cannot be deducted under Section 179 is real property, including buildings and their structural components. (Although there are some exceptions to that general rule, too.)

How Much Property Can Be Deducted Under Section 179?

Over the years, the maximum amount of the Section 179 deduction has gradually increased to $500,000 in Year 2014. This is a great way for small business owners to finally forget about depreciation and get a much bigger tax break right away -- in the year of purchase -- instead of waiting 5 or 7 years to get the tax benefits of equipment purchases.

The Tax Code had been increasingly generous to Small Business Owners over the past few years – note how the total cost of deductible Section 179 property has increased:

At first glance, the Section 179 deduction looks simple and straightforward. And for many small businesses, it is. But like most areas of tax laws, there are exceptions. What would a good tax rule be without a few good exceptions to the rule!

There are several exceptions to the Section 179 rule. Here are the two most important ones to keep in mind:

Exception #1: The Investment Limit

The Investment Limit is currently $2,000,000. If you purchase more than $2,000,000 of Section 179 property, then the amount of your Section 179 deduction is reduced as follows:

For each dollar of Section 179 property purchased over $2,000,000, reduce the maximum amount deductible by one dollar. So, if the cost of Section 179 property you bought during 2014 is $2,500,000 or more, you cannot take a Section 179 deduction.

IMPORTANT POINT: Obviously, most small businesses are unlikely to purchase over $2,000,000 or $2,500,000 of equipment in a single year, so chances are you do not need to worry about this Investment Limit.

EXCEPTION #2: THE TAXABLE INCOME LIMIT

The total Section 179 deduction is limited to the business' profit for the year. So if your annual profit is $105,000, you can deduct up to $105,000 of Section 179 property. If your profit is $10,000, you can deduct up to $10,000 of Section 179 property, and so on. If you just broke even or had a loss, you cannot take the Section 179 deduction.

Any cost that is not deductible in one tax year because of this taxable income limit can be carried over to the next tax year.

For some new businesses, this taxable income limit may apply. It is not uncommon for a new business to lose money in its early years, or to just break even. If that's the case, you may have to depreciate property until your business becomes profitable (sorry about that!).

OTHER IMPORTANT RULES REGARDING SECTION 179

There are some other critical rules governing the Section 179 deduction which are beyond the scope of this book. The primary purpose of this chapter is to provide an introductory overview of the concept, not delve into all the details. Many small businesses qualify for the Section 179 deduction for all their business property. If your business purchased equipment, please consult a tax professional to make sure you qualify for the Section 179 deduction.

And by taking advantage of this deduction, you gain two main benefits:

1. You avoid the complicated task of tracking depreciation;

2. You get to fully deduct the purchase price of property immediately. Why deduct something over several years when you can deduct it all right away?

CHAPTER 14. TAX-SAVING TIP #14 – HOW TO DEDUCT YOUR VACATION

Legal Loophole #14 can apply to all types of business entities: Corporations (both "C" and "S"), Partnerships, and Sole Proprietorships.

Over the years, tax law changes have made it increasingly difficult to deduct travel-related expenses. But there are still several legitimate deductions you can take for travel, so make sure you take advantage of the following items.

TRAVEL EXPENSES FOR BUSINESS TRIPS

The key to deducting travel expenses is this: What is the primary purpose of the trip? If the primary purpose is a business one, then you can deduct the cost of traveling to and from your destination, even if you stay a few extra days to enjoy pleasure-related activities. If the primary purpose is business-related, you can also deduct travel expenses even if you take a side trip for pleasure during the visit.

Here's an example: You travel to Chicago on Monday for a 5-day business conference which concludes on Saturday morning. After the conference is over, you decide to stay in Chicago for a couple more nights to enjoy the sights. Your travel expenses between home and Chicago are fully deductible (if you traveled by plane, the air fare is deductible; if you rented a car, the cost of the rental car plus gasoline; if you drove your own car, then you could take a mileage deduction or the actual cost of gasoline, depending on your particular situation). From Monday through

Saturday morning, you can deduct the cost of your lodging, local transportation and 50% of meals and business-related entertainment. After the conference is over, (from Saturday afternoon through your departure on Monday), the lodging, local transportation, meals and entertainment expenses are not deductible because that part of your trip was not business related.

WHAT ABOUT MIXING BUSINESS WITH PLEASURE?

Again, the key factor is the primary purpose of the trip. If you take a trip primarily for pleasure (like the traditional "family vacation"), then the cost of traveling to and from your destination is not deductible. This is the case even if you happen to engage in some business activity during the trip. But be aware that on a trip taken primarily for pleasure, you may incur some isolated business-related expenses that can be deducted.

Here's another example: You take a one-week vacation to Chicago. During the trip, you meet a customer (who happens to live there) for lunch. You can still deduct 50% of the meal, as long as business discussion occurred during the meal. Also deductible would be tax, tips, and parking-lot fees, as well as local transportation costs to get to the restaurant.

PLAN YOUR TRIPS ACCORDINGLY

With these rules in mind, make travel plans accordingly. When you go to another city on business, check out the possibility of staying a few extra days to play, especially if this is an area that you would likely travel to for vacation anyway. As long as the main purpose of the trip is business-related, you can enjoy considerable tax savings while enjoying a good time.

CHAPTER 15. TAX-SAVING TIP #15 – HOW TO TURN TAXABLE INCOME INTO TAX-FREE INCOME

Tax-Saving Tip #15 is available to owners of any type of business. In fact, you do not even have to own a business to implement this strategy -- but it is the best technique I know of to legally avoid income tax, so I could not resist including it in this book.

There is a perfectly legal way to turn taxable income into tax-free income. Technically, you do not even have to own a small business to implement this strategy. The vast majority of average, middle-class taxpayers can do this.

IRA's have been around for years. Many Americans have taken advantage of the Traditional tax-deductible IRA, which has been a great way to both save taxes and save for retirement.

Then a new type of IRA was created -- it's called the Roth IRA. This Roth IRA is how you can legally turn taxable income into tax-free income, and save literally thousands of dollars.

Roth IRA contributions are not tax-deductible. Instead, if the following two conditions are met, withdrawals from the Roth IRA are tax-free:

1. The Roth IRA owner is age 59 1/2 or older

2. The Roth IRA account has been open for at least five years.

The Roth IRA offers a very rare opportunity to receive TAX-FREE INCOME -- legally!

Remember this: Most Retirement Plan contributions (like employer-sponsored 401k and 403b Plans) and Traditional IRA contributions are tax-deductible now, and the growth of those contributions is also tax-sheltered while the funds remain in the account. But eventually all tax-deductible Retirement Plan contributions and all tax-deductible Traditional IRA contributions, as well as the growth of those contributions, will be subject to income tax when the money is withdrawn from the account.

In other words, Retirement Plans and Traditional IRA's offer the opportunity to postpone taxes. Retirement Plans and Traditional IRA's enable you to save taxes --- but these tax savings are temporary.

This is the big difference between Retirement Plans/Traditional IRA's and Roth IRA's:

Retirement Plans and Traditional IRA's allow you to temporarily postpone taxes.

The Roth IRA offers the opportunity to permanently avoid taxes.

For example: If you invest $2,000 per year for 20 years into a Roth IRA, you will have invested a total of $40,000. Now if that Roth IRA earns an average of 10% per year, that $40,000 will grow into $126,005.

Now comes the fun part: You can withdraw the entire $126,005 tax-free.

Remember though, you did not deduct the $2,000 per year of Roth IRA contributions -- these contributions were made with "after-tax dollars."

But the "growth" of your contributions is $86,005 -- and this entire $86,005 is tax-free income.

Now comes the really fun part! Had you put this same $40,000 into a tax-deductible Retirement Plan or Traditional IRA, you would have saved some taxes each year, and the annual earnings growth would have accumulated tax-postponed for 20 years. But when you withdraw the $126,005 during retirement, you will receive $126,005 of taxable income.

But since this $40,000 has been invested in a Roth IRA, you will end up paying literally thousands of dollars less tax. How much less tax?

Let's assume that you are in the 15% federal income tax bracket: $86,005 x 15% = $12,901

Assuming you pay 5% in state income tax, you would realize even more tax savings:

$86,005 x 5% = $4,300

NOTE: Your state and/or local income tax will likely be different than 5%. But I'm including the 5% in this example as a reminder that most folks do have state and local income tax, which should also be factored in to the tax-saving equation.

So, for taxpayers in the 15% federal income tax bracket,

the total federal and state income tax savings equals $17,201.

And if you happen to be in a higher federal income tax bracket, the savings are even more significant.

For taxpayers in the 28% federal income tax bracket, the total federal and state income tax savings equals $28,382.

Think about it: If you invest $2,000/year for 20 years in a Roth IRA instead of a Retirement Plan or Traditional IRA, you would end up paying $28,382 less tax -- during your retirement years. Don't you think that money will come in handy when you are retired?

Of course, understanding the advantages of a Roth IRA takes a long-term perspective. Many people may prefer to temporarily reduce taxes now (by contributing to tax-deductible Retirement Plans and/or Traditional IRA's) rather than permanently avoid taxes later. That's a personal decision that only you can make -- and it can be a very tough choice.

Other factors can come into play, too. The above examples assume that your federal income tax rate during your working years will remain the same during your retirement years. This may not be the case. For many people, their income is reduced during retirement years and so they find themselves in a lower tax bracket during retirement years.

EXAMPLE: If you make tax-deductible Retirement Plan and/or Traditional IRA contributions while in the 28% federal tax bracket, and then during retirement make taxable withdrawals in the 15% bracket, you will realize a permanent tax savings of 13%. So making tax-deductible contributions is not without merit in some situations.

Another situation that can compel one to contribute to an employer-sponsored Retirement Plan: many employers offer a matching program that rewards the employee for making tax-deductible contributions. These matching employer contributions can add thousands of dollars to your retirement savings -- money that you would not have received had you not participated in the Retirement Plan. Sure, you have to pay tax on this money when you make withdrawals many years later, but you are paying tax on free money -- money literally given to you by your employer.

So, there are several viable alternatives to choose from when saving for retirement. Unless you are independently wealthy already, you need to be doing something to save for retirement. Do you really think Social Security will be enough to live on 20 or 30 years from now? And fewer and fewer employers even offer the old-style employer-funded pension. And if your new business is your sole source of income, you are on your own to fund your own retirement. The SIMPLE Plan (discussed in Legal Loophole #8) is a great way to make tax-deductible retirement plan contributions. And the Roth IRA is a great way to make after-tax contributions that can turn into tax-free income.

Sorting out these options from a tax standpoint is a challenging task. In addition, you must also make retirement planning decisions from an investment standpoint. What is a Retirement Plan? What is a Traditional IRA? What is a Roth IRA? Are these primarily tax-related accounts or investment-related accounts? Obviously, they are both tax-related and investment-related.

Once you decide which kind of retirement savings account is best for you from a tax standpoint, you must then decide what kind of investment to put your contributions into. Now you really have some choices to make. There are literally hundreds of ways to invest your Retirement Plan and/or IRA money.

If you are comfortable making all these decisions on your own, great. But for many people, seeking the advice of a competent tax and investment professional can make a big difference.

CHAPTER 16. TAX-SAVING TIP #16 – HOW TO TURN EVEN MORE TAXABLE INCOME INTO TAX-FREE INCOME

More good news from Washington! Congress and the President have been passing laws that raise the maximum amount of money that you can contribute to a Roth IRA.

Over the years, the $2,000 annual limit has been gradually increased, and the maximum Roth IRA contribution is now at $5,500 for people under 50 and $6,500 for people 50 and older.

So, what does this mean for the self-employed person? It means that the amount of tax-free income you can accumulate (as calculated in the previous section) has been increased significantly.

If you take advantage of these increased Roth IRA contribution limits, the amount of tax-free income you can receive in retirement has been more than doubled. If you start putting $4,000 (instead of $2,000) into a Roth IRA for the next 20 years, go back to the numbers in the previous section and double them all. You'll get twice as much tax-free income, and your actual tax savings will be twice as much.

CHAPTER 17. TAX-SAVING TIP #17 – HOW TO PROCRASTINATE YOUR WAY TO TAX SAVINGS (PART I)

I've always liked that old saying, "Why do it today when you can put it off until tomorrow." When it comes to taxes, truer words were never spoken.

I'm not a big fan of paying taxes. Are you?

Not only do I dislike paying taxes, but I dislike having to pay taxes any sooner than necessary. Why pay taxes today when you can put it off until tomorrow?

But sooner or later, if you have taxable income, you are going to have to pay Uncle Sam. But at least there are some legal loopholes that allow you to legitimately postpone the payment of your taxes as long as possible, without any extra penalty or interest charges.

Think about it. It's your money. Yes, part of it has to go the government eventually. But until that time comes, why not hang on to your hard-earned dollars as long as possible? You get to earn more interest on your money, and you get to use that money for short-term cash flow needs.

Here's a little-known legal loophole that lets you wait all the way until April 15 to pay the final amount of tax due -- it's known as the Safe Harbor Method. Here's how it works.

Let's say you are doing some tax planning -- you are trying to figure out when to pay your income taxes for 2015. Let's further assume that for tax purposes your business is a Sole Proprietorship or a Partnership.

(NOTE: for Corporations, both "S" and "C", see Chapter 18, for additional tips on how to legally procrastinate the payment of taxes.)

Since you are a Sole Proprietor or Partner, you probably have to make quarterly estimated income tax payments via Form 1040-ES. And of course, in the government's infinite and wacky wisdom, these quarterly payments are due April 15, June 15, September 15, and January 15.

Rather than basing your quarterly income tax payments on projected or actual 2015 income, you can pay your Year 2015 tax based on your Year 2014 tax liability. You just go to your Year 2014 personal tax return, take the amount of federal income tax you paid for the whole year (your total annual tax liability, not the balance due), and divide that amount by four.

What you have just calculated is the minimum amount of federal tax you have to pay for Year 2015. It doesn't matter what your actual tax liability ends up being on the Year 2015 income tax return. During 2015, as long as you pay the Year 2014 tax liability amount in 4 equal installments, then you can wait until April 15, 2016 to pay the rest, without any penalty or interest.

This is a great strategy when your income goes up from one year to the next, for at least 2 reasons:

1. You get to keep some of your money until April 15 of the next year, giving you at least 3 1/2 months to earn interest

on that money or to use that money for other short-term needs.

2. You don't have to worry about figuring out exactly what your current year tax liability is going to be until after the year is over.

Keep in mind, of course, that this isn't such a great idea if your income decreases significantly from one year to the next. Why? Because then you end up paying in more than you were required (which I just absolutely hate to do). You'll end up getting a refund, but it just irritates me to let the government have more of my money than I'm legally required to give them.

So, if your income decreases substantially, then you shouldn't use the Safe Harbor Method. You are probably better off calculating your actually tax liability during the year and paying quarterly estimates based on those currently year calculations.

CHAPTER 18. TAX-SAVING TIP #18 – HOW TO PROCRASTINATE YOUR WAY TO TAX SAVINGS (PART II)

Now here is definitely one of the least-known legal loopholes I know of. Very few people know about this one, believe me.

Also, this loophole only works if you are a Corporation (either "S" Corporation or "C" Corporation). If you are a Sole Proprietorship or Partnership this loophole just won't work for you. Sorry! But this is yet another reason to form an "S" Corporation.

Here's how it works:

If you are a Corporation Shareholder/Employee, you can literally wait until the last day of the year to pay your taxes for the whole year. You simply wait until December 31 to create a paycheck for yourself. On this final paycheck, you can deduct your entire federal income tax liability for the year. Then the corporation will eventually pay this income tax withholding amount to the government via the Electronic Federal Tax Payment System (EFTPS).

Usually, small businesses have until the 15th of the next month to deposit employee withholding amounts. So the taxes withheld on December 31 would actually be paid to the IRS by January 15 of the next year.

You may be asking yourself a couple questions right now, such as, "How can I get away with waiting until the last day of the year to pay my taxes? Doesn't the government require me to pay-as-you-go?"

The answer to that question is, Yes, our tax payment system does operate on a pay-as-you-go basis. And most employees who work for a company must have taxes withheld from every paycheck. Generally, employees cannot wait until the last day of the year to pay their taxes. It just wouldn't work. Their gross wage amount wouldn't be enough to cover the withholdings, anyway.

Likewise, self-employed people (like Sole Proprietors and Partners) who make quarterly estimated tax payments also have to make equal payments throughout the year. The Safe Harbor method discussed in the previous section only avoids penalties and interest if the payments are made in equal amounts.

But as the Corporation's owner, you have much more control over your payroll system and your cash flow situation. So if you are in a position to do so cash flow-wise, you can wait until December 31, prepare one paycheck from which you withhold most (or even all) of your income tax for the year, and then pay it all at once by January 15th.

Here's why this is a perfectly legal loophole: This federal income tax which was withheld from your December 31 paycheck is reported on your Form W-2, which the Corporation will give to you as an employee. Specifically, it is reported on Form W-2 in Box 2, Federal Income Tax Withheld. No matter when the W-2/Box 2 amount was actually withheld from the employee's paycheck, the amount reported in W-2/Box 2 is treated as if it was withheld in equal installments throughout the year.

Do you see why this can be a great strategy for you to hang on to your money as long as possible? Again, assuming you can afford to wait this long, you can keep control of your money for many months before turning it over to the IRS. You could use the money for short-term operating capital, or just keep it in an interest-bearing account.

CHAPTER 19. TAX-SAVING TIP #19 – HOW TO LEGALLY AVOID TAX ON STOCK DIVIDENDS

You have probably figured out by now that I like "S" Corporation. For many Small Business Owners, it is definitely the way to go. You may be able to reduce your taxes by switching to an "S" Corporation, regardless of what kind of legal entity you currently own.

I'm the first to admit, however, that there are some advantages to legal entities other than the "S" Corporation. If you are a "C" Corporation, here's a great way to legally avoid tax. And believe me, there are very few times in the Tax Code when Uncle Sam lets you avoid tax. Most legal loopholes are able to help you reduce your tax, minimize your tax, or temporarily postpone your tax. But to avoid tax -- legally -- just doesn't happen very often in the tax code. Here's one time where it does occur, and it happens to apply to "C" Corporations only.

If your "C" Corporation owns less than 20% of the stock in another U.S. company, and that other company's stock pays dividend income to your "C" Corporation, then your "C" Corporation can avoid tax on 70% of those dividends. Not bad, eh?

The same type of rule also applies to companies in which your "C" Corporation owns 20% or more of the stock. It gets even better, though -- your Corporation gets to avoid tax on 80% of the dividend income from a "20% or more" company.

So if your "C" Corporation owns dividend-paying stock, be sure to take advantage of this legal loophole.

And if you own a "C" Corporation and are thinking about buying stock for your personal account, you should seriously consider having the Corporation purchase the stock.

What if you don't own a "C" Corporation? What if you own an "S" Corporation or Partnership? Sorry, there's no way to avoid tax on the dividends. The dividend income is reported on the tax return of the "S" Corporation or Partnership, but the business doesn't pay any tax on that dividend income. Instead, the dividend income is reported on each owner's Schedule K-1, and the end result is that this income is reported on the owner's personal income tax return.

So there is no tax advantage to owning stock in the name of an "S" Corporation or Partnership.

CHAPTER 20. TAX-SAVING TIP #20 – WHAT A DIFFERENCE A BRACKET CAN MAKE

Here is another potential tax advantage of the "C" Corporation. At certain income levels, the "C" Corporation owner may end up paying less income tax than the owner of a Sole Proprietorship, Partnership or "S" Corporation. Why is that? Let me explain.

First, keep in mind that these three other business types all pay the same amount of income tax on business profit. Here's why:

SOLE PROPRIETORSHIP

The Sole Proprietor reports business profit directly on his/her personal income tax return via Schedule C. End result: any business profit is subject to the Sole Proprietor's regular personal income tax rate.

"S" CORPORATION

Even though the "S" Corporation files a separate corporate income tax return (Form 1120S), the "S" Corporation ends up paying no corporate income tax on that Form 1120S. Instead, the "S" Corporation shareholders receive a Schedule K-1 from the corporation which reports each shareholder's proportionate share of the corporation's profit (or loss). The shareholder then reports the K-1 corporate profit on his/her personal income tax return. End result: the corporate profit is subject to the owner's regular personal income tax rate.

PARTNERSHIP

Same situation as the "S" Corporation, except the business return is called a Form 1065.   Each Partner receives a Schedule K-1. End result: Partnership profit is subject to the Partner's regular personal income tax rate.

And what are those personal income tax rates? Here's the personal income tax rates for Tax Year 2014 (assuming you file Married Filing Jointly): 10%, 15%, 25%, 28%, 33%, 35%, 39.6%. As your taxable income increases, so does your tax rate. To see how this works, click on the link below

http://taxfoundation.org/article/2014-tax-brackets

and go to "Table 1. 2014 Taxable Income Brackets and Rates".

Now, compare the above personal income tax rates to the "C" Corporation income tax rates, which happen to start at 15% and go all the way up to 39%. What is most important about these rates is that the "C" Corporation rate of 15% applies to the first $50,000 of corporate taxable income.

Now let's assume you are married (and filing jointly), and you are the only shareholder of a "C" Corporation which has $50,000 of profit. The corporation will therefore pay $7,500 of corporate income tax on that profit ($50,000 x 15%).

How much income tax would you have to pay on the $50,000 profit if you were a Sole Proprietorship, "S" Corporation, Partnership, or LLC? That's depends on the amount of taxable income you have from sources other than the business.

For example, let's assume your spouse is employed and has at least $73,800 of taxable income from that job. Now look at the personal income tax table. See how it works? The first $73,800 of taxable income is taxed at 2 different rates -- the first $18,150 is taxed at 10%; the next $55,650 is taxed at 15%, and then any taxable income above $73,800 is taxed at 25%. Your wife's $73,800 of taxable income puts you in the 25% tax bracket, and now all additional income above $73,800 will be taxed at 25%.

So, if you now add your $50,000 of business profit (from a Sole Proprietorship, "S" Corporation or Partnership) to your wife's $73,800 of taxable income, that entire $50,000 will be taxed at 25%. The end result: you pay $12,500 of personal income tax instead of $7,500 of corporate income tax. That's a difference of $5,000. And obviously, that's a big difference.

This subject of which business entity type is best can get complicated. The above example may or may not be applicable to your situation, and I did not include it to confuse you. Rather, I'm just trying to point out that at certain levels of income, you may end up paying less income tax as a "C" Corporation compared to the other business types.

Also keep in mind that the above example assumes that the "C" Corporation shareholder did not need (or want) to distribute the $50,000 as dividends. Instead, the "C" Corporation chose to retain the profits in the business, perhaps to fund expansion or provide operating capital. Had the "C" Corporation made a $50,000 dividend payment to the shareholder, then that $50,000 would be taxed again on the shareholder's personal tax return -- and so be subject to the dreaded Double Taxation of Corporate Profits discussed in Chapter 6.

CHAPTER 21. TAX-SAVING TIP #21 – HOW TO PAY LESS TAX ON AN EARLY RETIREMENT

Many Small Business Owners have retirement plan and/or IRA assets that they would like to access during the early years of their business. For example, you might have been an employee for a larger company for many years prior to starting your own business. You've built up quite a nest-egg in that company's retirement plan over the years, and now you've decided to go it alone.

While your new business is getting started, you may need to access your retirement plan or IRA funds to make ends meet. Hey, don't feel bad! Many new business owners (and even experienced business owners) have cash flow crunch times, when the business just isn't making enough money to support the owner.

So there sits your retirement plan or IRA. Sure, you hate to dip into the money you were going to reserve for your Golden Years, but sometimes this may be your only option, or at least it may be the best option available to you. Again, don't feel bad -- it happens.

One of the major disadvantages of taking money out of your IRA or retirement plan is simply this: any withdrawals will be subject to income tax. There is no way to avoid this. The money you put into the traditional IRA or tax-deductible retirement plan was not subject to income tax, and all the growth of your contributions has legally avoided income tax while in the account, so when you take money out of the account, the withdrawals are considered taxable income.

A second major disadvantage of an IRA or retirement plan withdrawal has to do with how old you are. If you are younger than 59 1/2 years old, the withdrawal is considered an early withdrawal or premature distribution, and as such it is subject to an additional 10% penalty. Ouch.

There are several exceptions to the 10% early withdrawal penalty, for both IRA's and retirement plans.

For IRA's, the exceptions include withdrawals made due to death, disability, certain health insurance premiums for the self-employed, higher education expenses, first-time home purchase, certain medical expenses, and an IRS tax levy.

For employer-sponsored retirement plans like a 401k, the exceptions include withdrawals made due to death, disability, retirement after age 55, medical expenses, and an IRS tax levy.

There is another exception to the 10% early withdrawal penalty that applies to both IRA's and retirement plans. It is known as The Substantial and Equal Periodic Payment exception. Sometimes it is also referred to as the Annuity Exception or Section 72(t) Withdrawal.

Here's how it works:

You can receive distributions from your traditional IRA or retirement plan that are part of a series of substantially equal payments over your life (or your life expectancy), or over the lives (or the joint life expectancies) of you and your beneficiary, without having to pay the 10% additional tax, even if you receive such distributions before you are age 59 1/2.

You must use an IRS-approved distribution method and you must take at least one distribution annually for this exception to apply. The easiest method to use is generally referred to as the "Life Expectancy Method." This method, when used for this purpose, results in the exact amount required to be distributed, not the minimum amount.

There are two other IRS-approved distribution methods that you can use. They are generally referred to as the "amortization method" and the "annuity factor method." These two methods are not discussed in this book because they are more complex and generally require professional assistance. See IRS Notice 89–25 in Internal Revenue Cumulative Bulletin 1989–1 for more information on these two methods. This notice can be found in many libraries and IRS offices.

Here is the most important thing to understand about this Substantial and Equal Periodic Payment rule:

The payments under this exception must continue for at least 5 years, or until you reach age 59 1/2, whichever is the longer period.

So, once you have determined how much you must withdraw each year, those withdrawals must continue for at least 5 years, and perhaps longer than 5 years if you are younger than 54 1/2.

Example: You are 45 years old and want to begin taking withdrawals from your IRA without paying the 10% penalty. You have to take these equal payments until you are 59 1/2 -- which means you have to receive these IRA withdrawals for 14 1/2 years.

Example: You are 58 years old and want to begin taking withdrawals from your former employer's 401k plan without paying the 10% penalty. You have to take these equal payments for 5 years.

If the payments under this exception are changed before the end of the above required periods for any reason other than the death or disability of the IRA owner, he or she will be subject to the 10% additional tax.

If you are looking for a way to take money out of your IRA or retirement account without paying the extra 10% penalty, this is the way to go!

CHAPTER 22. TAX-SAVING TIP #16 – HOW TO SAVE TAXES BY OWNING AND LOANING

Most small businesses get their operating capital from one primary source – you. As a Small Business Owner, you have probably poured not only your heart and soul into this business, but also a sizable amount of cash -- cash to get things going, pay the bills, and so on.

If you have borrowed money from a bank, you probably had to put the loan in your own name rather than the name of the business. Even more likely is this scenario: if you were unable to come up with the cash from your own resources (savings accounts, retirement plans, credit card advances, etc.), you probably then went to family and friends to get the rest of the operating capital you needed to finance your business.

Now comes the important question: What about all that money you've poured into the business? How is it treated for tax purposes? Do you have to pay that money back? Or can it just stay in the business forever?

The answer to these questions depends on what type of legal entity your business happens to be. Here's an overview:

Sole Proprietorship. If you are a Sole Proprietor, you can put your own money into the business whenever you want and pay yourself back whenever you want. It really doesn't matter. Whatever profit you have (as reported on your personal income tax return via Schedule C) is subject to income tax and self-employment tax, no matter how much of your own money you had to contribute to the business to make it profitable.

Corporation.   Here's where things get much more interesting. Since the corporation (both the "C" Corporation and the "S" Corporation) is a separate legal entity from the owner(s), it is much more critical that you document all loans between you and the business.

It is a big mistake to just indiscriminately put money in by paying business expenses out of your own pocket (which is a common mistake made by many small business owners whose business happens to be a corporation).

If you provide operating capital to the business, it is much better to put the money directly into the corporation's checking account, then pay the bills out of the corporation's checking account.

Each time you put money in like this, you should treat this money as a bona fide loan between you (the shareholder) and the corporation.

What do I mean by a bona fide loan? I mean have the business treat this loan just like a loan that you could get at a bank.   For example, a true loan has the following characteristics:

1. A written loan document or note agreement.

In other words, put it in writing. Would a bank loan money to your business without putting it in writing? Of course not. The loan agreement simply states the terms of the loan: when the loan is to be repaid, what the interest rate is, etc.

2. An interest rate that reflects current market conditions.

3. A written corporate resolution which authorizes the loan.

4. Collateral for the loan.

If there is no collateral, then the interest rate should reflect that.

5. Evidence that the loan has indeed been repaid.

In other words, treat the transaction as a true arm's length transaction between two willing parties.

Now, why is all this paperwork so important? For the simple reason that once you have loaned money to your business, eventually the loan must be repaid. Those repayments are a very critical source of tax savings to you. Once the business starts making a profit and has the cash flow to repay the loan, you can then start paying yourself back what the company owes you. Instead of paying yourself wages, which are taxable income to you, you can pay yourself back the loan, which will be non-taxable.

I've personally seen several situations in which the business owner had loaned the company literally tens of thousands of dollars over the years. Then, the business owner never directs the corporation to pay back the loan. Instead, the business owner pays himself wages or salary with money that could have been classified as loan payments. The result: the business owner needlessly pays income tax and payroll taxes on those wages. Had those wages been treated as loan payments, taxes would have been legally avoided.

CHAPTER 23. TAX-SAVING TIP #23 – HOW TO SAVE A BUNDLE BY JUST BEING ON TIME

As a Small Business Owner, you either already have employees or will eventually have employees (assuming your business continues to grow). And even if you are a one-person band, if you have formed a corporation (or plan to do so soon), then you have at least one employee – you.

Having employees (even just one) means having to make payroll tax payments and file payroll tax returns. There are very strict rules regarding when to make these payroll tax payments. These payroll tax payments are due at the federal, state, and even local level. For purposes of this discussion, I'm going to focus on the federal payroll tax payments.

The most common federal payroll tax is known as the Form 941 tax. This is a combination of the following 5 types of federal payroll tax:

1. Federal income tax which you, the employer, have withheld from your employee's paycheck

2. Employee's Social Security tax which you, the employer, have withheld from your employee's paycheck

3. Employee's Medicare tax which you, the employer, have withheld from your employee's paycheck

4. The employer's share of Social Security tax. You have to match whatever has been withheld from your employee's paycheck.

5. The employer's share of Medicare tax. You have to match whatever has been withheld from your employee's paycheck.

So items #1, #2 and #3 come out of the employee's pocket. Items #4 and #5 come out of the employer's pocket. After withholding all these payroll taxes, the employer is required to pay these taxes to the federal government, usually on a monthly basis.

Here's how it works. The IRS determines how frequently you must pay Form 941 tax by adding up all the payroll taxes you have paid over a recent 12 month period. If your total Form 941 tax is less than $50,000 for that 12 month period, then you have to pay the Form 941 tax every month. If you total Form 941 tax is greater than $50,000 for that year, then you have to make payments within a few days after each payday.

What happens if you make a late payment of Form 941 tax? The penalties are harsh, as evidenced in the following table:

2% - Payments made 1 to 5 days late.

5% - Payments made 6 to 15 days late.

10% - Payments made 16 or more days late. Also applies to amounts paid within 10 days of the date of the first notice the IRS sent asking for the tax due.

15% -   Amounts still unpaid more than 10 days after the date of the first notice the IRS sent asking for the tax due or the day on which you receive notice and demand for immediate payment, whichever is earlier.

In addition to these late payment penalties, the IRS will also add an interest charge based on the actual number of days the payment is made late.

So, it is extremely important that you treat payroll tax payments as a top priority. It is easy for a new (and perhaps struggling) business to overlook payroll taxes. Maybe things are tight and you are having a hard time paying your bills. So you borrow from Peter to pay Paul, so to speak, by taking the amount of withheld payroll taxes from your employee's paychecks to pay other bills, or to just have some money to pay yourself.

The end result -- you now owe Uncle Sam even more than the original payroll tax you withheld, because now a couple months have gone by and an additional 10%, 15%, or 20% of penalty and interest charges have been added to the bill.

I've seen this happen to many small business owners who thought they could ignore their payroll tax payments when things got tough. They seem to think that if they just don't pay Uncle Sam, he will go away. Unfortunately, it doesn't work that way. The IRS will start sending you late payment penalty notices like you wouldn't believe.   Month after month they will arrive, while the penalty and interest charge clock continues to tick every day.

Meanwhile, the business owner just continues to ignore these notices -- maybe he's still having trouble making ends meet, and now that the IRS has added literally hundreds or even thousands of dollars in late penalty and interest charges, well, it's now even more difficult to pay the IRS and get caught up.

Please don't let this happen to you. Stay on top of your payroll tax situation -- make all required payments on time, and you will save yourself alot of time, trouble, and your hard-earned money.

CHAPTER 24. TAX-SAVING TIP #24 – HOW TO DEDUCT 100% OF YOUR BUSINESS MEALS

Business Owners have been able to deduct at least a portion of business-related meals for many years. Currently the deduction is limited to 50% of the cost of the meal.

What many Business Owners do not realize, however, is that there are exceptions to the 50% Rule that allow you to deduct the full cost of your business-related meals. You just have to know how these rules work, so here's an overview:

An employer can usually deduct the cost of furnishing meals to employees (including the owner) if the expense is an ordinary and necessary business expense. In general, the deduction for furnishing meals is limited to 50% of the costs except under certain conditions

Deduct 100% of the cost of furnishing meals for:

1. Meals that qualify as a de minimis fringe benefit. This includes all meals provided on the employer's premises for the convenience of the employer if more than 50% of the employees who are furnished meals are furnished meals for the employer's convenience. Prior to 1998, substantially all of the meals provided to employees had to be for the employer's convenience.

What is a de minimis fringe benefit? It is a benefit provided to an employee that has minimal value. An example of a de minimis fringe benefit would be something like occasional personal use of office equipment by the employee. Such de minimis fringe benefits (like the cost of furnishing meals to the employee on the employer's premises for the convenience of the employer) are deductible by the employer and tax-free to the employee.

2. Meals where the value is included in the employee's wages.

3. Meals furnished to employees at the site of an employer's restaurant or catering service.

4. Company picnics or holiday parties.

The important thing to realize here is that the value of meals is excluded from an employee's wages when the following requirements are met:

1. Meals must be furnished on the business premises

2. Meals must be furnished for the convenience of the employer

Meals that can be excluded from an employee's wages under the exclusion rules are treated as de minimis and are fully deductible by the employer. If more than half the employees that are furnished meals meet the exclusion rules, all meals provided to employees are treated as de minimis and are fully deductible by the employer and are excludable to the employee.

A key part of the loophole is the phrase "for the convenience of the employer". Just exactly what does this mean? To meet the employer's convenience rule, meals must be provided to the employee for one of the following reasons:

1. Meals are provided so employees are available for emergency calls during the meal period, and such calls actually occur or can reasonably be expected to occur.

2. Meal periods must be short (30 to 45 minutes) because of the nature of the employer's business and the employee does not have time to eat elsewhere. Short meal periods to allow employees to go home early do not qualify.

3. Because of a lack of eating facilities near the business (or other similar circumstances), employees cannot be expected to secure proper meals within a reasonable meal period.

4. Meals furnished to restaurant or other food service employees during working hours.

5. Meals furnished immediately after working hours that would have been provided during business hours but because of work duties, were not eaten during working hours.

CHAPTER 25. TAX-SAVING TIP #25 – HOW TO DEDUCT VIRTUALLY ALL YOUR VEHICLE MILEAGE

Business Owners have always been able to deduct expenses related to the use of their vehicles. Obviously, if the business owns the car, and the car is used 100% for business purposes, then all vehicle-related expenses are deductible, including:

1. The cost of the vehicle, as deducted each year via depreciation expense

2. The actual cost of gasoline

3. The actual cost of maintenance, repairs, oil changes, etc.

4. Automobile insurance

5. Vehicle registration and license plate fees

6. Emergency road service membership fees such as AAA Auto Club

But for many Business Owners, it is more common that the business does not own the car. Rather, the Business Owner has purchased a vehicle in his or her own name, but then uses that vehicle for business purposes. The Business Owner can then deduct vehicle-related expenses only to the extent that the car is used for business. So, you must maintain a written log of your business use miles, and at the end of the year you either deduct the appropriate business use percentage of the actual expenses listed above, or you deduct an expense equal to the number of business miles times the prevailing mileage rate established by the IRS. For Year 2014, for example, the mileage rate is 56 cents per mile.

For many Business Owners, the Mileage Rate Method provides a higher deduction than the Actual Expense Method. So here's an easy (and perfectly legal) way to substantially increase the number of miles that you drive your car for business purposes.

First, you must realize that commuting miles are not counted as business use miles. When you get in your car and drive to your place of business, even when you own the business, this commute is considered a non-deductible personal use of your car.

But there's an easy way to get around the commuting rule. Simply create an office in your home (and for many Small Business Owners, you probably have already done this). Then, start each day by first going to work in your home office.

The tax code says that driving from home to your place of business is a non-deductible commute. But the tax code also says that driving from one business location to another (second) business code is deductible business mileage. So, driving from your home office to your place of business is no longer a commute. It is driving from one business location to a second business location. This enables you to legally deduct the cost of your commute because now it is no longer a commute.

Here's an example of how you can save money by implementing this legal loophole. Assuming the distance between your home office and your place of business is 15 miles each way, you would get to deduct an additional 7,500 miles per year:

15 miles one-way x 2 trips per day = 30 miles per day

30 miles per day x 5 trips per week = 150 miles per week

150 miles per week x 50 weeks per year = 7,500 miles per year

And what is that 7,500 miles worth to you?

7,500 miles x .56 = $4,200 deduction

And depending on your tax bracket, what is that deduction of $4,200 worth to you in actual tax savings? Let's assume you pay about 28% federal income tax and 5% state income tax for a total income tax rate of 33% --

$4,200 x 33% = $1,386 in actual tax savings.

So, this simple record-keeping technique could save you over $1,300 per year. Over the next 10 years, that would be over $13,000 of extra cash in your pocket.

CHAPTER 26. TAX-SAVING TIP #26 – BE IT EVER SO DEDUCTIBLE, THERE'S NO PLACE LIKE A HOME OFFICE

One of the most under-used and over-looked deductions is the infamous Home Office deduction. A few years ago, the IRS got tough on how it interpreted the complex set of rules governing this deduction, and so many deserving Small Business Owners were no longer allowed to take this deduction. And even those who still qualified were scared off by the IRS tough stance.

But I have good news for you. A provision in the Taxpayer Relief Act of 1997 makes it easier for many taxpayers to claim the home office deduction.

Prior to 1999, the home office deduction was only available to taxpayers who could meet the strict interpretation of the principal place of business requirement. Now it is much easier to qualify.

Here's how it works: The area used for business in your home must be used regularly and exclusively:

1. As the principal place of business (including administrative use); or

2. As a place to meet or deal with clients/customers in the normal course of the business; or

3. In connection with the business if it is a separate structure not attached to the taxpayer's personal residence.

Now, for some definitions of the key terms used above:

Regular Use: The area used for business is used on a continuing basis. The occasional or incidental use of the area does not meet the regular use test, even if it is used for no other purpose.

Exclusive Use: A specific part of a taxpayer's home is used for business purposes only.

Here's how the deduction is calculated:

1. Determine the Business Use Percentage by dividing the area exclusively used for business by the total area of the home.

2. Add up all of the following Home-Related Expenses which benefit both the business and personal parts of the home. These expenses involve the upkeep and running of the entire home:

Mortgage interest

Real estate taxes

Homeowner's insurance

Security system

Home repairs & maintenance

Utilities

Rent

Depreciation

Water, sewer, garbage removal, snow plowing

3. Multiply the Home-Related Expenses by the Business Use Percentage.

The end result is that the typical Small Business Owner who spends time in his Home Office gets a substantial business deduction for expenses that he would have paid for whether or not he used part of his home of business. This is truly one of the best deductions available to the Small Business Owner. Make sure you are taking it.

CHAPTER 27. TAX-SAVING TIP #27 – IT IS BETTER TO GIVE THAN TO RECEIVE

Charitable contributions have been deductible by both individuals and businesses for many years. The government has always given a nice tax break to those taxpayers with the means and desire to help others.

But for individuals, here's an important rule to consider: You only get to deduct your personal charitable contributions if you itemize deductions on Form 1040, Schedule A. So if you don't have enough itemized deductions to file Schedule A, then you are out of luck. Your charitable contributions will provide you with no tax benefit whatsoever.

If you happen to own a "C" Corporation, here's a great way to get around that problem:

A "C" Corporation can deduct up to 10% of its taxable income as a charitable contribution. So, if you are not able to deduct your charitable contributions on your personal return, then just make sure you use your business checking account (instead of your personal checking account) to write the checks for your charitable contributions.

Here's another great tax deduction for "C" Corporations involving charitable contributions of property (as opposed to contributions of cash). By property, I mean inventory held for resale and depreciable assets.

The tax code allows a "C" Corporation to donate inventory to charity and deduct more than the cost of the inventory. The amount of the deduction is equal to the cost of the inventory item plus one-half the difference between the cost and the regular sale price (aka "Fair Market Value"), up to twice the cost of the inventory.

Here's an example of this little-known legal loophole that let's you buy something and then deduct more than what you paid for it:

ABC Corporation buys a product for inventory at a cost of $500. Normally, ABC Corporation has a 100% markup on the product and so normally sells it for $1,000. Therefore, the Fair Market Value (FMV) of the inventory is $1,000.

ABC then donates the property which it bought for $500. But ABC gets to deduct $750, because the amount of the contribution (for tax deduction purposes) is $500 (cost) plus $250 (one-half of $500, which is the difference between cost and FMV).

To qualify for this "greater than cost" charitable contribution, the following rules must be met:

1) The charity must be a Section 503(c)(3) organization

2) The charity must use the donated property solely for the care of the ill, the needy, or infants

3) The charity cannot exchange the donated property for money, other property, or services

4) The corporation must be given a written statement from the charity that says it will follow rules (2) and (3) above

5) If the donated property is subject to the regulations of the Federal Food, Drug, and Cosmetic Act, all such regulations must be satisfied

6) Use of the donated property must be related to the purpose or function that gives the charity its exempt status.

CHAPTER 28. TAX-SAVING TIP #28 – SAVE THOSE RECEIPTS!

I regularly receive email from sincere folks who ask questions like this: "Is it true? If I don't have good records, will I really pay more tax than I could/would/should have?"

Or how about this one: "If I don't have receipts, does it really matter? If I get audited, will the IRS nail me for not substantiating my deductions?"

The answer to every one of those questions is an emphatic "Yes!" And if you think I'm just making this stuff up to scare you, well, think again. And here's the proof that the IRS does really nail the average Joe for not having receipts.

I'd like you to meet an average Joe, although his name is really Mike — Michael Robert Cottrell. Mike was self-employed and made about $5,700 in self-employment income one year. He didn't report that income because he thought, "I have at least that much in expenses, so my expenses offset my income and I really didn't make any profit. So there's really no need to report the income or the expenses."

Well, the IRS audited Mike, and when the IRS told him to prove those deductions with a paper trail, Mike was unable to do so. He literally had no records whatsoever to document his claim that his net profit was zero.

He admitted to receiving the $5,700 in income, but then proceeded to claim that about 50% of that income was spent on materials, 25% went toward subcontracted labor, and the rest went to pay other miscellaneous expenses and debts.

The IRS said, "Prove those deductions." Mike said, "I don't have any records. They were lost when I moved." The IRS said, "Sorry, Mike. No receipt, no deduction."

End result: the IRS nailed Mike with a tax bill to the tune of $1,625. Because he didn't have any written record of his deductions, his deductions were disallowed.

There you have it. It does happen. And it can happen to you, if you choose to Be Like Mike.

NOTE: The information about Mr. Cottrell is a matter of public record — Michael Robert Cottrell T.C. Summary Opinion 2003-162.

Yes, there are a few exceptions to the "No Receipt / No Deduction Rule". For example, you can deduct your vehicle expenses based on mileage rather than actual expenses. This is known as the Mileage Rate method, and you do not have to keep receipts to use the Mileage Rate method.

Another exception involves meal receipts when using the Per Diem Method and is explained in Chapter 29.

But generally speaking, it's best to cultivate the habit of keeping your receipts and filing them in a well-organized record keeping system. Otherwise, you take the risk of running afoul of the IRS, and that will not bode well for you on Audit Day.

CHAPTER 29. TAX-SAVING TIP #29 – CARPE DIEM: SEIZE THE PER DIEM METHOD (AND THROW AWAY YOUR RECEIPTS)

As I just explained in Chapter 28, the mantra of tax record-keeping has remained relentlessly burdensome for decades: "No Receipt, No Deduction".

But fear not, you who loathe the never-ending climb up the mountain of paperwork required by the U.S. tax code. Many of our most beloved tax rules have exceptions, and such is the case with this one.

Believe it or not, there are actually expenses you can legally deduct without a receipt. Here's one for self-employed folks who travel out-of-town on business.

When it comes to deducting your meals while on an overnight business trip, you have two options with regard to record-keeping.

OPTION #1:

You keep your receipt from each meal and simply deduct the cost of the meal times 50%, a la the "No Receipt, No Deduction" rule.

OPTION #2:

You use The Per Diem Method to determine your meal deduction. For each day of the trip, you are allowed a daily meal allowance, depending on what part of the country you were visiting.

For example, the per diem meal rate for Birmingham, AL is $56. For San Francisco, it's $71.

Like Option #1, your actual deduction is 50% of the per diem amount -- $28 in Birmingham and $35 in San Fran.

To find the per diem allowances, go to IRS Publication 1542 – Per Diem Rates (For Travel Within the Continental United States).

If a particular area is not listed, then the allowance is $46 per day.

Take note: There are two very nice advantages to The Per Diem Method.

Benefit #1: You don't have to keep receipts for your meals. Yep, you can pitch 'em. Scouts honor.

Benefit #2: It doesn't matter how much you actually spend on meals, you still get to deduct 50% of the per diem amount. This can result in hundreds of dollars in tax savings for you.

Example:

You regularly go to several cities for overnight business trips, traveling about five days each month. These cities all have a per diem rate of $51.

You are frugal. To save both time and money, you prefer to eat at fast food restaurants three times a day. On average, you spend only $20/day on meals.

But the per diem rate is $51/day. If you used Option #1, your actual deduction would be $20 x 50%, or $10/day. With Option #2, you get to deduct $51 x 50%, or $25/day.

The difference between Option #1 and #2 is $15/day. Over the course of the year, this adds up to an extra $900 in deductible meal expenses ($15/day x 60 days) -- even though you didn't actually spend the $900.

End result: you save $315 in taxes (assuming your combined federal and state income tax rate is 35%). And you can throw away 60 days of meal receipts.

So you get $315 in tax savings without spending a dime.

One final note: The per diem method is available to Sole Proprietors and Partners. If your business is a Corporation and you own more than 10% of the company stock, you can't use the per diem method for yourself. Sorry! That's taxes for ya.

VALUABLE COUPONS WORTH $150

Don't forget that as a reader of this book, you are entitled to redeem Tax Coupons valued at $150. Click on the link below to access the coupons. This is my way of saying "Thanks" for reading this book, and to make sure you get your questions answered by a tax professional with over 25 years' experience.

Coupon #1 – Free 30-minute phone consultation. You get to talk with me and ask me any questions you have about the tax deductions explained in this book, in case you need clarification or just want to make sure you understand how to apply them to your particular situation.

Coupon #2 – Free review of your most recently filed tax returns (Business and Personal). I can take a look at your tax situation and let you know if there are any deductions you've overlooked, and I can also tell you the tax savings you'll get by putting these tax deductions to work.

Don't let these coupons just sit here! Use them, and use them right away! Thousands of dollars in tax savings could be waiting for you if you take action and redeem these coupons.

Click here to access the Tax Coupons worth $150 -- www.selfemployedtaxdeductionstoday.com/tax-coupons.pdf

RECOMMENDED RESOURCES

This book is just the tip of the Tax World iceberg. There are many other excellent books on taxes for Small Business Owners and the Self-Employed. Here are three of my favorites.

Schedule C Tax Deductions Revealed:
The Plain English Guide to 101 Self-Employed Tax Breaks
By Wayne Davies, EA (I know, I'm plugging own book.)
www.amazon.com/dp/B01AMB97SM

Do you know the #1 tax question asked by self-employed people? "What's deductible?"

Do you know where to find the answer? Right here.

With easy-to-understand, "plain English" explanations, best-selling author Wayne Davies takes you line-by-line through Schedule C and reveals over 101 legitimate tax deductions for sole proprietors.

No technical gobbledygook. No fancy jargon that only a tax lawyer can understand. This book is written for you, the typical self-employed person who needs straightforward, practical advice on what you can deduct that will reduce your taxes, put more of your hard-earned money in your pocket, and allow you to sleep well at night – without any fear of an IRS audit.

If you're self-employed (either full-time or part-time) and need help knowing what's deductible, this book is for you. Freelancers, consultants and small businesses of all shapes and sizes will benefit from the no-nonsense information provided. If you're an independent contractor and report your business as a sole proprietorship, you need this book to make sure you're not missing out on the deductions you're entitled to take.

Small Business Taxes Made Easy:
How to Increase Your Deductions, Reduce What You Owe, and Boost Your Profits
By Eva Rosenberg, EA
www.amazon.com/dp/0071743278

In my opinion, Eva Rosenberg (aka "TaxMama") is the best Tax Teacher on the planet. She has not only written an excellent book on taxes for small business owners, she also runs a first-class website and newsletter, is a syndicated national columnist, and teaches tax professionals how to study for and pass the rigorous Enrolled Agent (EA) exam. I am one of her students. I took Eva's EA Exam Review course, and I would never have passed the EA exam with her help!

For more info about Eva and the many tax resources she offers, visit www.TaxMama.com

Here is my review of Eva's book "Small Business Taxes Made Easy" that I posted on Amazon.

"This book does exactly what it promises to do. Nothing could be more complicated that the wild and wacky world of business taxes. This book definitely makes understanding business taxes significantly easier. This is because Eva Rosenberg is a gifted teacher and writer -- she has the unique ability to take a complex subject and explain it in a way that makes sense. I've been reading Eva's articles and newsletter content for the past 7 years. I've attended her webinars and online classes. She really knows her stuff, and she takes what she knows and gives it to you in this book like she's sitting across the kitchen table and laying it all out for you.

So do not view the title and sub-title as marketing hype. If you own a small business or are thinking about starting one, or if you are self-employed or thinking about going solo, get this book and get a tax education you desperately need. You won't be disappointed. You will learn how to increase your deductions, reduce your taxes, and increase profits."

Lower Your Taxes - Big Time!
By Sanford Botkin, CPA
www.amazon.com/dp/0071849602

This is another great book. Here's my Amazon review.

"Sandy Botkin is one of America's top tax reduction specialists. I purchased a set of his audio CD's about 5 years ago on tax reduction strategies for small business owners and self-employed people and it was awesome. Well, he's managed to take virtually all the info from those CD's and put it in this book.

This guy is a tax deduction machine-gun -- in rapid-fire manner, he spews forth one great tax-saving deduction after another. He used to work for the IRS as an auditor, and he's also a CPA, so he's one of the most knowledgeable tax experts I've ever encountered, and I've been preparing tax returns for a living for the past 20 years.

If you want to get your hands on practical tax-saving advice, get this book. I guarantee you'll find at least 10 or 20 or 30 (or more) tax deductions that you've never heard of before, or maybe you've heard about them but really didn't understand the finer points. Sandy will explain it all to you in an easy-to-understand writing style. He's a good communicator and has the knack for explaining difficult concepts in a way that non-accountants can understand."

ABOUT THE AUTHOR

WAYNE M. DAVIES, EA has been doing individual and business tax returns for 25 years and has personally prepared over 10,000 tax returns.

Wayne specializes in providing tax reduction strategies to small business owners and the self-employed, including home-based business owners, freelancers, consultants and solo entrepreneurs.

For more of Wayne's tax-saving strategies, you can subscribe to his free weekly small business tax newsletter at www.SelfEmployedTaxDeductionsToday.com

He also provides accounting and payroll services for all business types, as well as year-round tax planning.

You can contact Wayne at 260.480.7545 or via email at wayne.davies@supervalu.com

You can also connect with Wayne on Facebook at www.Facebook.com/GoodTaxPreparer

ONE LAST THING...

If you enjoyed this book or found it useful I'd be very grateful if you'd post a short review on Amazon. Your support really does make a difference and I read all the reviews personally so I can get your feedback and make this book even better.

If you'd like to leave a review then please click below to visit the Amazon.com page for this book and scroll down to "Customer Reviews".

http://www.amazon.com/dp/B00RW169CI

Thanks again for your support!

45628134R00075

Made in the USA
San Bernardino, CA
30 July 2019